What Others Are Saying . . .

"A refreshing professional, humane interface between the practitioners of the law and those entering their first contact with the legal system. A very readable must."

—*David R. Metcalf, M.D.,Psychoanalyst*

"Highly successful New Mexico trial lawyer Merit Bennett has written a fine book about the need for the legal profession to connect with the heart. Merit's book seeks to understand why we lawyers are held in such low esteem by our clients, and offers a basis to repair our badly damaged relationships.

To help us understand legal relationships better, Merit draws on a variety of psychological and spiritual traditions and analyzes how the mind relates and perceives relationships with others. It is essential that we understand how all of these processes work in order to begin to heal the legal relationship.

The foundation of this healing is the compassionate heart. It's time for the heart to be brought into the legal profession."

—*Grove Burnett, Director, Western Environmental Law Center*

"*Law and the Heart* was both interesting and full of excellent advice and commentary about lawyer-client relationships. I want to give a copy of the book to my son, who is just beginning his own private practice. I am sure he will benefit from it. I wish that such a book had been available to me when I first started law practice. Thanks for giving the profession this fine book."

—*Daniel H. Benson, Professor of Law,*
School of Law, Texas Tech University

"Merit combines his lawyer's acumen and his personal insight to remedy an area of ignorance in the legal profession — a domain where relational dynamics have traditionally bypassed the heart and where lawyer and client are driven by unconscious power needs rather than bonds based on mutual trust and a shared search for equity." —*Elaine Simard LaForet, Jungian Analyst*

LAW

Heart and the

A Practical Guide for
Successful Lawyer/Client Relationships

by
MERIT BENNETT, J.D.

LIBRARY OF CONGRESS CATALOG CARD NUMBER: 96-077235
ISBN: 1-57282-000-4

Cover design by Janice St. Marie
Book design by James Berry

Cataloging-in-Publication Data
174   Bennett, Merit.
BEN   Law and the heart : a practical guide for successful lawyer /
        client relationships / by Merit Bennett. - Santa Fe, N.M. : The
        Message Co., ©1997.

           168 p. ; cm.

           Summary: Examines why lawyers no longer have the esteem
        of their clients and outlines a more humane approach to the
        legal process, by which the damaged lawyer/client relationship
        can begin to be repaired.

           ISBN 1-57282-000-4

        1. Attorney and client   2. Law - Moral and ethical aspects
        3. Lawyers - Conduct of life 4. Legal ethics I. Title

                                                    174'.3_dc20

Published and distributed by:
The Message Company
4 Camino Azul
Santa Fe, NM 87505
505-474-0998

Printed in the United States of America.
Printed on acid-free recycled paper using soy ink.

Acknowledgments

The love, support and insight of my wife, Dori, and my family, Talia, Grant, Colin and Kelsey, have been invaluable to me in the conception and writing of this book. They continually remind me to look inward. I am especially grateful to Dori and Talia for their editorial help.

This book is dedicated to the honor of my teacher, Gangteng Tulku Rinpoche.

I am also grateful to my dedicated and skilled assistant, Douglas Gould, who cheerfully processed many drafts of the text and had many helpful suggestions. A special thanks goes to Ron Schultz who extended his editorial expertise to me in selfless friendship. Thanks also to my friend, Foster Perry, who sparked my self-rediscovery, and to Dave Metcalf, Jerome Bernstein and Josie Josephson-Gibb who helped me keep it going. And thanks to Rudi Holscher who believed in me.

Finally, I am very grateful to all of my clients who have helped me understand how lawyers can provide a better service.

The Liberated say that just as God is the stay of the universe, so also, the Heart is of the individual. The part must be of the nature of the whole; the Whole (God) is Infinity. Therefore, there is no distinction between the Heart and God.

   —Ramana Maharshi, Indian saint, *Collected Works of Ramana Maharshi*

Table of Contents

Page

Introduction   1

1 How the Mind Relates   7
Projection   9
The Reflection   14
The Shadow   17
The Witch   22
Shame   26
The Victim   31
Sex and Gender   36
Denial and Rationalization   40
Many Voices   44
The Corporate Mind   48
Competition   53
The Hero Warrior   58

2 Taking Responsibility   63

3 Entering the Lawyer-Client Relationship   69
Clarifying Intent   69
   Disputes   70
   Agreements   75
   Technical Compliance   80
Choosing a Lawyer   84
Choosing a Client   88
Boundaries and Ground Rules   92

4 Relationship through the Heart 99
The Essence of Legal Relationship 100
The Role of the Heart 103
Emotions and Feelings 107
Conflict and Anger 110
Forgiveness 116
Choices 121
Attitude 122
Thoughts 125
Words 131
Action 135
Measuring Success 141
Sacrifice and Service 145

5 Where to From Here? 149

References and Suggested Reading 153

Introduction

Why is there always a secret singing
When a lawyer cashes in?
Why does a hearse horse snicker
Hauling a lawyer away?
—Carl Sandburg, from "The Lawyers Know
Too Much"

Lawyers are in trouble. Their clients cannot relate to them. They are perceived as uncommunicative, lacking in compassion and undeserving of trust and confidence. Essentially, people feel that lawyers lack integrity.

In a recent public opinion survey by the American Bar Association, the majority of those polled viewed lawyers as less caring and compassionate than lawyers in the past, and barely one in five people said the phrase "honest and ethical" described lawyers. The survey suggested that the more people had contact with the legal profession, the lower their opinion of lawyers. This poll graphically documents the decline in the stature of the legal profession.

This book seeks to understand why lawyers no longer have the esteem of their clients and how lawyers and clients can begin to repair their badly damaged relationships.

The technological direction of our society has correspondingly required more legal technocrats, and the services of lawyers as philosopher-counselors are generally considered to be an archaic impediment to commercial progress. As society has increasingly venerated the rational mind and discounted the feeling and intuitive nature of humans, so has the legal profession attracted to its ranks those who lost access to their own feeling or intuitive selves in childhood.

1

The dangers of this trend are as obvious as the crisis in the legal profession is now apparent. When the law is separated from the feelings that are associated with its application, the results reflect the disconnection: shady or dishonest dealing, pollution of the environment, economic oppression and, of course, "public distrust of lawyers".

It would be a mistake for the non-lawyer reader to assume that only lawyers need to explore and develop access to their feelings and intuition. Our culture teaches all of us from a very early age to stay in our heads, that "logical" and "rational" is preferred over "sensitivity" and "feelings." "Stop crying and be tough!"

This cultural predisposition is also gender neutral. Girls at a young age are encouraged to emphasize their intellects over their feelings if they are to successfully compete with the boys. Our limited cultural view generally associates feelings and emotions with the female gender, and it is therefore no wonder that the cultural tendency to discount feelings is reflected in our culture's relegation of females to non-leadership roles. Women are the physical representatives of the emotional bodies that men were taught to reject.

Even though clients are upset with the legal system and have their own horror stories to recount and lawyer jokes to tell, they share some responsibility for their plight. In order to restore a positive connection between the law and the feelings of the people operating within it, clients can learn how to recognize the limitations of the rational mind and to positively assert their own feelings and intuitive common sense in their relationships with lawyers.

No matter how much we dissect the legal system and attempt to improve it through a reform of its organizational structure, its successful functioning depends upon its capacity to encourage integrity in its human relationships. Effective change can never occur unless the participants in the system begin to learn how to relate to one another honestly through feelings and intuition as well as through the intellect. The premise of this book is that the survival of the healthy and positive benefits of our system of justice depends upon how well we, both lawyers and clients, consciously and intuitively expand our awareness of the intrinsic laws of human relationship. The only way the legal system can change for the better is from the inside out, by transforming the way lawyers and clients relate to each other, by understanding the mind's habits and by re-introducing intuition through the feeling heart.

Once we become aware of our mind's habitual and automatic tendencies, we can turn to the task of discerning how we really feel. Until we fully develop our conscious capacity to feel what we feel, we will not have the ability to respond in our legal relationships in a complete or meaningful way. In order to recognize our feelings and follow them to our intuition, it is helpful to know how our minds work so we do not confuse our feelings with emotions that are evoked by habitual thought patterns.

In this book, we will search for access to that part of our being that connects us to higher wisdom, the source that knows what is best for us from a comprehensive or total perspective. We also sometimes refer to this link-up with our individualized divinity as our intuition. Our feelings are what we experience within our body when our intuition is activated. Carl Jung believed that our feeling self is that voice within us that places value on each of our life experiences. This valuing process can actually be measured by our body, and when we are directly connected with our higher knowledge, we feel "right". When we are not, our body physically reacts with revulsion to the disharmony. Often mistaken for our feelings, our emotions describe the nature and quality of the energy that our feelings generate. Typical emotions are fear, anger, sadness, guilt, happiness and love.

According to Jung, our intuition is that part of us that can put our feelings into a larger context which synthesizes our past and present experience. We often refer to intuition as a "hunch".

Many speak of the heart or the gut as the repository of this faculty. We sometimes describe the phenomenon of an intuitive insight as a message that comes to us from outside of the body, "out of the blue", or at the very least from a place that cannot be easily understood by our rational mind. Whatever the specific source, it is that part of us which knows our own unique truth, even though it may defy our mind's logic and be contrary to our conditioned beliefs or the popular consensus.

If we want to take more responsibility for the course of our legal relationships, we must begin to cultivate our intuitive abilities by first listening and responding to our feelings. Our feelings can help us value the quality of our present experience without digressing into abstract reasoning. When our mind quiets, our intuition can shoot the gap and unfold our feelings into a larger perspective. Once we experience the power of our intuition to transcend the mundane, we can start making legal decisions which are more consistent with who we really are and who we really want to be.

Tuning in to our feelings requires acknowledgment that they are in there, somewhere, and that they are somehow available to us. This may be a challenging task for those of us who learned at an early age that our survival depended upon keeping our feelings to ourself. Some of us rationalized our silence by adopting the belief that feelings were for sissies or that they indicated mental deficiency or inferiority. The answer for many of us was to stop feeling, or at least convince ourselves that there was nothing to feel. When someone now points out that we might be feeling something, most of us immediately deny the possibility and actually believe ourself. So if we really want to change our behavior and feel what we feel, we may need an intense re-education.

This re-education process may mean that each of us will have to acknowledge the existence of a "spiritual reality". Even though I do not emphasize the spiritual context of intuition in this book, it is ever present, and each reader must come to his or her own terms with it. The "New Age" movement has usually floundered when its lofty spiritual principles become a substitute for a day-to-day commitment to correct dysfunctional habits in our inter-personal relationships. This book reflects such a commitment, yet is always mindful that the larger context has esoteric dimensions.

I will first examine some of the tendencies of the mind when engaged in human relationship in order to demonstrate the need for the balance of our feeling nature, and I will then explore ways to effectively access our inturition through our feelings in the context of lawyer-client relationships.

This is a complicated subject, and by no means is this book intended to provide simple solutions. I write to suggest that the reintroduction of feelings and intuition into legal relationships can positively transform the legal system itself.

> Law reform is far too serious a matter
> to be left to the legal profession.
> —Leslie Scarman to New York City Bar
> Association, January 1955

1

How the Mind Relates

If you think that you can think about a thing,
inextricably attached to something else, without
thinking of the thing it is attached to, then
you have a legal mind.
—Thomas Reed Powell, lawyer, law school
dean and legal writer, recalled on his death
in 1956

Our meddling intellect
Mis-shapes the beauteous forms of things:-
We murder to dissect.
—William Wordsworth, from "The Tables
Turned"

Our examination of legal relationships begins with our mind and
how it perceives relationship with others. When I use the term
mind, I am referring to that part of us that makes a distinction
between who we are and everyone else, between subjects and
objects, between past and future. My reference to "mind" limits
the term to the functions of our brain which interpret our experience to conclude that we are separate and distinct physical
organisms which interact over time with a physical world in
accordance with rules which are derived through analysis of
empirical data.

Many of us believe that we *are* separate from the physical
world that we perceive through our senses and that we interact
with that world in accordance with objective physical laws. Our
minds are therefore conditioned to view relationships in terms
of independent participants relating through their physical senses
instead of as interdependent parts of a larger whole relating on

non-physical, as well as physical, levels.

What follows is a discussion of some of our mental tendencies that can unconsciously fashion belief systems which predictably determine the quality of our legal relationships.

When we consciously understand how the mind works, we can begin to transform the dynamics of legal relationships that repeatedly result in disappointment or failure.

Projection

We can say that no aspect of our experience,
of the outer phenomenal world or the inner
mental world, has one atom of reality.
Nothing we experience is anything more than
the mind's perception of its own projections,
the reality of which is only conventional.
— Kalu Rinpoche, Tibetan Buddhist master,
    from *The Dharma*

Is this a dagger which I see before me,
The handle toward my hand? Come, let me
    clutch thee:
I have thee not, and yet I see thee still.
Art thou not, fatal vision, sensible
To feeling as to sight? or art thou but
A dagger of the mind, a false creation,
Proceeding from the heat-oppressed brain?
— William Shakespeare, from "Macbeth"

When clients walk through the doors of my office for the first
time, they usually arrive with their minds stuffed with precon-
ceived ideas about lawyers and the legal process. When they sit
down in front of me, they peer at me through their mental images
of how things ought to be. From that point on, almost everything
I say or do will usually be interpreted by the client according to
the client's perception of how the legal process functions and how
I am supposed to act.

I have had many clients come into my office for the first time
and expect me to be a legal barracuda. I was expected to be
openly aggressive and to utilize any means necessary to advance
their cause. Some clients have even verbalized their assumption
that I will be dishonest for them so long as I get paid. They automatically assume that I exactly match their perception that

9

lawyers have no conscience.

Likewise I developed a mental picture of what to expect from the average client. When I met some of my clients for the first time, I assumed that the preferences of the person sitting in front of me would not significantly deviate from those of the average client faced with a similar legal challenge. The natural tendency of my mind to sort through my past experiences and arrive at a common experiential denominator has often caused me to treat the unique human being sitting before me as just another replica of the common denominator and to ignore anything to the contrary.

Many times, assuming that my client understood my routine rap, I neglected to explain certain legal concepts in detail, only to discover later that my failure to communicate clearly caused me to embark on a path that jeopardized my client's legal interests. I have also often assumed that my client would agree with my judgment and the legal alternative I would choose if it were me, only to learn that my judgment was misplaced, and the ultimate legal consequences were inconsistent with my client's desires.

So long as we remain unaware of our mind's natural tendency to re-experience only what we have previously experienced, we will continue to encounter our own pre-determined beliefs, instead of the one-of-a-kind individual sitting across from us. This phenomenon of encountering our own mind when relating with another person is called "projection".

We all have had at least one experience of projection. Remember when other people assumed that we should feel a certain way because they would have felt that way under similar circumstances? Or they assumed that we would take a certain course of action because they would have taken that course of action if they were in our shoes?

These are projections. The other people were projecting onto us their own way of relating to the world. In other words, the other people did not see *us*, they only saw themselves and how they would feel or act in our place.

Or remember when we ran into an old friend that we had not seen for a long time, and we noticed how uncomfortable they were because we had changed? We were not the same person that they knew before, and they did not know how to comfortably relate to this "new" person. The reason for the discomfort was that the old friend had carried around in his or her brain an image of who we were when we last parted, and when we did not fit the image, there was discomfort or awkwardness. This is a projection. Our friend "took a photograph" of who we were years ago and carried it around in his or her pocket all that time. When we met again, our friend started talking to the photograph of who we were supposed to be. After further exposure to the new us, our friend may develop a new photograph, but initially the tendency is for our friend to deal with us as if we were the old photograph and assume that *essentially* nothing had changed.

Let us go a little deeper with this. The "photograph" itself is a projection. When the friend took this mental "photograph" of us and who we were as a person years ago, the friend was really taking a photograph of who the friend thought we were at that time based upon how the friend viewed the world and based upon how different or the same we appeared to be from our friend's viewpoint. In other words, our uniqueness was determined by our friend whose definition of uniqueness was determined by his or her perception of reality. Therefore, our friend's initial judgment about who we were years ago was a projection that was later re-projected when our friend saw us again. Neither projection represented exactly who we were at the time; the first one just seemed to fit better.

Taken even further, we are all projecting our view of how reality works onto others all the time because that is all we know. It is difficult to know who another person really is because our own mind colors our perception.

It may be disconcerting to realize that what we "know" to be reality is a projection of our own mind on an "outer" world. However, we can choose to be inspired by this knowledge and make meaningful changes in our legal relationships by becoming more conscious of how projections work. If our perception of reality is the projection of our own minds, it follows that we can change our perception by changing our projections. And we can change our projections by changing the attitudes or thoughts that cause us to view the world in a certain way. It may not be an easy task to reverse a lifetime of conditioned behavior, but the power to make any change ultimately rests within each one of us.

We can also change the quality of our legal relationships when we acknowledge that our perception of who others are or how they relate to us is, to a large extent, determined by the way we choose to see them. For example, if we believe that people who wear black shoes are not to be trusted, our belief may be confirmed every time we meet someone wearing black shoes because we project onto them our predisposition of mistrust, whether or not they deserve it, and we may interpret everything they do or say to be consistent with our beliefs. They may actually become someone whom we cannot trust, and we can point to plenty of "objective" facts to prove it.

This can become even more difficult to sort out when the projection is made from our unconscious past. For example, if we had a father who was cruel to us when we were a child, we may unconsciously project our suppressed anger toward our father onto male authority figures in our adult life, such as a boss or a lawyer. Our relationships with these men can therefore predictably trigger our anger or resentment. We can unconsciously project this anger toward father onto men in authority positions even though we consciously say we love our father very dearly. Alice Miller, in her book *For Your Own Good*, convincingly argues that parents' acts of cruelty are often interpreted by their children to be acts of love. In our example, if a male authority figure, such as a lawyer, abuses his power and acts cruelly toward us, we may mistakenly interpret that cruelty to be an act of caring and continue in the relationship because we have projected onto our lawyer our childhood perception of conduct that we believe to be consistent with love.

Once we know how the process of projection works, we can begin to examine the projections we make in our legal relationships and how they originate. Only then can we begin to change our projections and thus change our experience of our legal relationships and their ultimate consequences. Some of us may be able to actually experience and perceive our projections in progress. Some of us may not be so fortunate, and we may need the aid of a trained therapist who can help us catch ourself in the act of projecting so we can understand how our mind creates and recreates a habitual and non-spontaneous reality. I was solidly in the latter group, but with good coaching, I am slowly getting better at detecting when and how I project my beliefs onto my clients, at least those beliefs that would impair my ability to communicate more clearly about the consequences of each of their available legal options.

Although projection is only one facet of our reality which is defined by the synchronistic and interconnected arising of phenomena in our field of experience, an understanding of how we project our view of reality onto others is essential to the process of healing the lawyer-client relationship. Later in this book we will discuss ways to ameliorate the impact of projections which weaken the lawyer-client relationship, and suggestions will be offered that may insure legal decisions based upon information gleaned from our internal reality, not from our external projections.

The Reflection

Everything that irritates us about others
can lead us to an understanding of ourselves.
—Carl Jung, from *Memories, Dreams,
Reflections*

When lawyers and clients project their respective beliefs of how the legal world ought to be onto each other, it naturally becomes difficult for each to discern the real person from the projected belief. Lawyers proceed at great risk when they assume that their client shares the same values as all other clients represented by the lawyer in the past. We often see lawyers barging ahead with a course of action that their client finds too heavy-handed or otherwise inappropriate. When this occurs, the lawyer is usually unaware that the action being taken is unauthorized unless the client verbalizes a contrary reaction. Before the client actually expresses a reaction, the lawyer often assumes that the client is reflecting back to the lawyer nothing inconsistent with the lawyer's concept of what the client wants. In any event, either the client's silence or verbal feedback can provide the lawyer with invaluable information about how accurately the lawyer's representation of the client is manifesting the client's intent.

In my law practice, I often fail to notice subtle signals from my clients which could reveal that the approach I am taking is not going to be appropriate for the success of our relationship. On other occasions, when I relax my rigid projections, I am able to see my present state of consciousness reflected back to me by my clients. For example, their distrust of me or of the legal system can mirror back to me my lack of compassion for their feelings of alienation.

Carl Jung and many other Western thinkers fundamentally

agree with the Eastern understanding that every person with whom we come in contact reflects back to us who we are at that particular point in time. What we may see in another person is a projection emanating from ourself, because our perception of what defines the other person is often dependent upon us as a point of reference. Most of us tend to define other people in terms of our own personal experience and therefore find it difficult to imagine that they might be different from the picture painted by our thoughts. In other words, we simultaneously project ourselves onto them and interpret our projection in terms of us. What we see may be part of us whether we want to claim that part of us or not. The meaning of the reflection we get back from others remains hidden from our awareness unless we consciously work to understand that what we see could be part of who we are. We are generally attracted to people who reflect back to us those aspects of ourself that we consciously accept. We usually reject people who reflect back those parts of ourself that we dislike and therefore deny and suppress.

The reflection may not necessarily be a precision image. That is, we may not always see another exactly *duplicating* or *imitating* our present behavior or state of being. The reflection of who we are may also be deduced from how the other *responds* to our state of being or to our behavior.

For example, when we are willing to say "yes" to anything because we want to be liked, other people may reflect back our willingness by taking us at our word and enlisting our help for projects that we never really want to undertake. Our submissive view of life can cause a predictable response in the other person. If we carefully examine the other person's response to us, we may see ourself more clearly.

The reflection back to us can also indicate that a change in our behavior or our belief system is warranted. In our example, if we continually find ourselves saying "yes" to everyone's request for help with their projects, we may consider that saying "no" would give us more time for our own projects and that we deserve to say "yes" to ourself.

A reflection can also help us transform the behavior that causes another person not to want to relate with us. If we really want to associate with someone, yet cannot understand why the feeling is not mutual, we may be able to discern from their dislike for us the nature of our habitually offensive behavior. Our usual responses to people who dislike us may range from feeling inferior to angrily dismissing them, but if we work with the concept that another person's behavior toward us is often a reflection of and caused by our own behavior, perhaps we can make adjustments in our behavior that can lead to more desirable relationships.

Reflections teach us that what goes around does come around. This is equally true in lawyer-client relationships. Clients can say "yes" to a lawyer to their inevitable detriment because they feel they should pay deference to the lawyer's training and expertise. Many times this misplaced deference will be reflected back to the client in a result which is not totally harmonious with the client's wishes. Lawyers, too, can unwisely defer to clients and then have to deal with the reflections of clients who cannot appreciate a reasonable resolution of their legal dilemma nor the lawyer's advice to accept it. In either case, the reflection can be changed only by a change in the behavior of the person upset by the reflection. If the change in behavior is not accomplished early on in a lawyer-client relationship, either the relationship will terminate on less-than-amicable terms, or the road to the conclusion of the relationship may be long and tortuous.

The Shadow

Everything that we see is a shadow cast
by that which we do not see.
— Martin Luther King, Jr., from *The Measure
of the Man*

Every part of our personality that we do not
love will become hostile to us. We could add
that it may move to a distant place and begin
a revolt against us as well. . . . Shakespeare's
poetry is marvelously sensitive to the danger of
these inner revolts. Always the king at the
center is endangered.
— Robert Bly, from *A Little Book on the
Human Shadow*

Most of the clients whom I have represented over the years have
asked me at some point to agree with their negative opinion of
another person, organization or governmental agency so that I
could advocate their legal position with the "proper" frame of
mind. Early in my career, I would usually join in their negative
judgment and give them aggressive legal advice that would enable
them to prevail in a conflict with their actual or potential
adversary.

When I was growing up, it was always easy for me to find fault
with others because they irritated me or threatened my sense of
well-being. I never considered that what I did not like in them
was identical to what I did not like in me. I also would never
have guessed that I could be projecting an aspect of me onto
another person.

After practicing law for many years, I began to notice that the
following scenario would unfold in my office with unwanted frequency.

A client would come to my office and tell me that someone or some group was causing the client to suffer harm. The client's story would usually be couched in a way that would portray the person or people purportedly causing the harm in an unsavory or negative light. The "doer" was invariably painted as a "wrong" doer.

My usual response would be to assume that the client's assessment of the sinister motives of the perpetrator was accurate, and I would immediately begin to devise legal strategies designed to defeat or, at least, to neutralize the "evil" opposition.

The results of most of these crusades against the "dark forces" were uncomfortably similar. I would often spend a considerable amount of my time and my client's money in the name of righteous indignation only to finally realize that our opponent was not as bad as we initially had thought.

After I had gone down this path many times, the light finally began to dawn. I had been literally fighting against myself. When I began to put aside my "holier-than-thou" attitude and accept that in my life I had done most of the reprehensible things that the "wrongdoer" was accused of, I was then better able to help my client to have some compassion for the "wrongdoer" and to accept some measure of responsibility for how and why the "wrong" got done. This approach has since proven to be much more successful. In many instances, what would have usually been a legal crisis of monumental proportions became instead a manageable and resolvable situation which was far more satisfying and far less costly.

When my clients and I projected our dark or shadow sides onto an evil wrongdoer, we were usually projecting those parts of our psyches that we did not want to claim as part of who we were. It was easier for us to unite against a bad guy than take a critical look at ourselves.

Many have attempted to explain how and why the mind does not want to claim its not-so-nice thoughts. Carl Jung was the first to clearly describe the nature and power of this psychological phenomenon. Robert Johnson's book, *Owning Your Own Shadow*, is one of the best recent works concerning the shadow. Robert Bly's writing and poetry also provide an excellent complement to the psychological discussion of this dynamic in contemporary relationships.

From the day we were born, many of us were told that certain ways we expressed ourselves were "bad" or "unacceptable" or "impolite" and that we should not act or be that way again. We were conditioned to hide parts of ourselves in order to be "good", "accepted" or "polite". As we grew up, our closet of unwanted skeletons got bigger because we felt compelled to meet all of the narrow expectations of parents, teachers, spouses and national and local customs. More and more of what we did or said was labeled as "wrong" or "bad".

Our skeleton closet is a metaphor for the unconscious. After being conditioned to put aspects of who we are into our closet, we actually forget who we really are—at least in our conscious, waking lives. We believe that we cannot possibly be associated with the skeletons who live in our closet, and we therefore cannot tolerate people around us who seem to possess our skeletal attributes.

One of the reasons we react negatively to certain people may be because we are projecting onto them a characteristic (or characteristics) of our own personality that lives in our closet, and then we judge it on the other person in the same way we were judged when we decided that it was better to keep that part of ourself out of sight. We may also judge others in the same way we were taught to judge ourself. This is learned behavior, not divine morality. We can actually, and usually unconsciously, reenact the judging behavior of the person who originally judged us because that is the only way we know how to act or react when someone else is behaving as "badly" or as "wrongly" as we supposedly did.

So, two things may be happening simultaneously whenever we evaluate another person or their actions in qualitative terms such as good or bad, right or wrong, acceptable or unacceptable, appropriate or inappropriate, beautiful or ugly, etc. First, we may be projecting an aspect of ourself that has been negatively judged onto another person as if the other person actually possessed that attribute in every moment of his or her life; or second, once we have the projection securely fitted, we may then judge the reflection of that projection back to us in the same way that attribute was judged in us. It is no wonder that we see dysfunctional family abuse patterns passed unconsciously from generation to generation. The cyclic patterns of these projections may be all we know, because we have nothing but our own experience to draw from.

Shadow projections can run rampant in legal relationships. For example, it is not surprising when a client projects onto his or her lawyer the client's disgust for someone who appears assertive, because the client was taught that assertiveness is unacceptable behavior. Nor is it surprising when a lawyer projects onto a client the lawyer's disdain for someone who appears confused, because the lawyer was shamed as a child when he or she became confused.

Shadow projection does not only refer to the projection of personality characteristics that are judged negatively. It includes the projection of attributes that are judged to be positive. Behavior that was nurtured and approved by parents, siblings or other authority figures can also be unrealistically projected onto a person who may not live by that positive attribute all the time. In other words, we may allow ourselves to unrealistically trust a person whom we deem to possess one or more attributes that we think deserve great praise, such as always saying the right thing, always appearing to know what they are talking about, always taking charge and giving orders. With a positive shadow projection, the tendency may be to give up our personal power to people whom we perceive to have positive attributes because, for example, we were expected to say the right thing, to appear to know what we are talking about and to take charge and give orders. This misplaced admiration can result in a client unrealistically projecting crusading knighthood onto an aggressive lawyer or a lawyer mistakenly projecting wisdom onto an assertive client.

When we understand our shadow and how it affects our legal relationships, we can begin to relate to people, not projections, and we can begin to reintegrate and gently reintroduce these ghosts of our former self back into our being in ways that can empower us and lead us to more compassionate legal decisions.

This integration process is, of course, very tricky business and may require our long-term commitment. If we simply act out our shadow without tempering it with compassion, our reclaimed shadow material may still be misdirected. For example, instead of reclaiming assertiveness just to define our boundaries, it could be used aggressively to violate the boundaries of others.

Carl Jung believed that we cannot become conscious of our shadow without considerable moral effort. When we are willing to invest the necessary moral effort in our legal relationships, we can begin to pull back our shadow projections and stop blaming others for our legal dilemmas. The less we see others in a negative or adversarial light, the less we will chase our shadows to costly legal conclusions.

The Witch

SECOND WITCH: By the pricking of my
   thumbs,
Something this way wicked comes.
Open, locks,
Whoever knocks.
MACBETH: How now, you secret, black, and
   midnight
hags!
What is't you do?
WITCHES: A deed without a name.
   —William Shakespeare, from "Macbeth"

The shadow projection of the archetypal witch deserves special attention because an understanding of this dynamic is a key to the honest expression of our feelings in our legal relationships. The power of the witch can best be illustrated by a personal experience.

At one point during my law practice, I had five women clients who were involved in various stages of legal conflict with others. To my knowledge, these women did not know each other, but they all had one thing in common: they were impossible clients. They were angry and bitter and in no mood to peacefully resolve their legal situations. They would back away from what I thought to be reasonable settlement opportunities and would constantly complain to me about the progress of their cases and my increasing bills, which they were not inclined to pay. They would not respond to my standard "Mr. Nice Guy" attitude and would ignore my advice to settle their disputes even to their own advantage. My representation of each of them was very time-consuming, frustrating and ineffectual, and I had little hope of getting paid for my efforts. My attempt to win their approval and cooperation did not impress them, and everything I did or suggested only increased their rancor toward their adversaries and toward me.

When all of these relationships simultaneously reached a legal and personal crescendo, I happened to read Robert Bly's *A Little Book On the Human Shadow.* Bly writes about how we give up our personal power by projecting our unclaimed inner witch onto figures in the outer world who then angrily make ever-increasing demands of us. Bly explained that this relinquishment of power can be reversed when we reclaim our positive witch, the energy that asserts what we know is right for us, and reintegrate it into our own being, instead of letting it angrily manifest in others whom we then condemn as being "bitchy" or tyrannical.

This book was a revelation. I knew instantly that my positive inner witch had negatively relocated in my five clients because I had failed to claim her as part of myself. In doggedly choosing the role of "Mr. Nice Guy", I had given up my power to say "No!" to other people. I had become boundary-less and would easily give up what was right for me in order to accommodate someone else's view of "rightness" and gain their acceptance and approval. Obviously, my abdication of the ability to assert myself was not serving me with these particular clients. My witch was on the loose, and she was angry because I had been neglecting her.

Immediately after reading this book, I began to consciously reclaim my witch in my professional relationships with these women. I began setting boundaries which more realistically reflected my true desires. I began to say "no" in situations where I used to say "yes" even though I had really wanted to say "no". I began to use phrases like "that's not right", "I don't agree with that", "that doesn't feel good to me", "that's unacceptable to me." I began to reclaim my positive witch energy by firmly expressing to these clients how I really felt about the unnecessarily contentious decisions they were making.

Within a month, my five challenging clients left my life. Four of the cases were settled, and the fifth client thankfully went to another lawyer.

I had dramatically experienced how my outer and inner worlds were directly connected. When I regained the strength of my inner witch, she no longer had to nag me into awareness by manifesting in the form of a haggling relationship in my outer world.

How many times in our lives do we say "yes" and feel "no"? How many times do we defer to other people because they appear to be stronger or more assertive than us or because we want them to like us?

This scenario is typical of many lawyer-client encounters. Many people will defer to a lawyer's proposed strategy or legal solution simply because the lawyer appears to be speaking from a position of authority, and the client does not feel empowered enough to say "no" even though the client may have serious doubts about the wisdom of the course of action the lawyer is recommending. When the client feels this way, the client is encountering his or her own "witch", which now resides in the breast of the lawyer. By deferring to the lawyer even though the client's inner voice says "this doesn't feel right", the client is rejecting his or her positive witch who then is reflected back to the client as a negative shadow projection. Scorned, she then makes the client regret the projection and leads the client through a painful outer world experience.

Clients can learn to say "no" or at least to ask hard questions when their feelings do not agree with the mental and, of course, exceedingly logical legal solutions suggested by their lawyer. Clients can trust that their expression of feelings in the face of an otherwise rational and seemingly unassailable legal construct will demonstrate time and time again the power of the positive witch. Clients can usually *feel* when a proposed solution will actually work when it is implemented. It therefore helps to speak up when there is a contrary feeling.

As with my fortuitous personal experience, lawyers can also give voice to their feelings of what is right as well as what is "legal." Many lawyers suppress their expression of what feels right for fear of offending the fee-paying client who is looking for a quick legal "fix". As a result, the lawyer may manipulate the law to yield legal solutions which do not feel right even though they can always be impeccably rationalized.

Just as clients can honor their feelings by reclaiming their witches, lawyers can say "no" to clients when they refuse to be reasonable or when they want to turn a quick economic or emotional profit at the expense of others.

Shame

The tragedy of life is what dies
inside a man while he lives.
—Albert Schweitzer, recalled on his death,
September 4, 1965.

Some people use shame to goad others into a course of action which is often inconsistent with the true feelings of the one who capitulates. Many legal relationships are driven by shame. In my early days of law practice, I could be easily shamed into remaining silent in the face of criticism from a client or from another lawyer. All either had to do was intimate that I might be making a mistake in judgment, and my fear of being humiliated would cause me to doubt my own feelings and deferentially seek the approval of my critic. I was especially vulnerable when a prospective client would imply that I was not man enough to tackle his or her legal problem. This tactic would immediately evoke feelings of shame, and I would recklessly stick my neck out for some pretty questionable legal causes. My shame could even be triggered in the absence of criticism, because my fear of being criticized would often encourage me to anticipate and therefore avoid any possibility of embarrassment.

Although shaming behavior is prevalent in many legal relationships, the grand arena of shame is the courtroom where shaming is routinely employed by lawyers as a deliberate technique to discredit witnesses. Because the physical reaction of someone feeling shame is similar to the physical response of someone who has been caught in a lie, many trial lawyers attempt to invoke shame in a witness in order to portray the witness as a liar.

When we are born, our mind cannot easily distinguish between our outer world and our inner reality. We often personally iden-

26

tify with those people in our environment who assume responsibility for our support and education. Our mind allows these parental or authority figures to define who we are or, at least, to determine whether who we are is acceptable or unacceptable. When our expression of who we are is judged negatively by any of these people, we can experience shame. Shame is a belief that the unique essence of who we are is unworthy of praise and sometimes even deserving of punishment. The two best books dealing with shame that I have found are *Healing the Shame That Binds You*, by John Bradshaw, and *Shame, The Power of Caring*, by Gershen Kaufman.

When we are shamed to the core of our being, we usually continue to experience the sensation of shame every time another person directs similar judgment our way. In fact, we can interpret innocuous remarks or unintentional conduct of others to be critically judgmental because we cannot imagine that we deserve anything better. This propensity to experience shame can follow us throughout our days and can cripple our capacity to enjoy life fully. We can become bound by our shame.

The emotion that usually accompanies shame is anger. Even though our mind believes the shame to be true and identifies with it, the feeling part of us knows that we are not our shame and can be angry with our acceptance of it. Because many of us encounter shame at an early age before we have learned any defenses to it, we cannot easily express the anger that knows it is not true. In fact, we quickly learn that any effort to defend ourself against shame will usually be met with swift and sometimes severe punishment. So our mind is often conditioned to silently accept shame as our lot in life, and our unexpressed anger builds and settles deep into our unconscious as smoldering rage, rage at the shamer for shaming and rage at ourself for allowing it to happen.

When we are children, our mind naturally compares objects, people and experiences in order to secure our place in the world.

During this developmental process, we may sometimes have difficulty discriminating between comparisons that define who we are and comparisons that diminish who we are. When we adopt a shaming comparison as part of the definition of who we are, we usually shame ourself with it long after the original shaming event has occurred. We can also become addicted to the physical and emotional sensations that accompany our shame and either trigger it ourself or pair in relationship with another person who can oblige our unconscious craving.

We can also inherit shame from parental or authority figures who have been shamed themselves. Even though these prominent figures in our lives may quietly carry their own burden of shame and not actively pass it on to us, we can still acquire the feeling of shame through our unconscious participation in their cover-up of their own shame.

Most shame, however, is dynamically transferred to others. When we learn at a young age from our primary role models that shaming is an integral element of how humans relate to one another, we are likely to unconsciously reenact what we have learned when we later create our own relationships. We can be taught by the example of our role models that the way to lighten our own burden of shame is to unload it onto our relationship partners.

Many of us also know how to devise strategies for avoiding new shame. Instead of confronting shame that is directed toward us and pointedly declaring our unwillingness to accept it, we may become generally defensive and dodge it by denying that we have committed the crimes of which we are accused. In other words, we allow shaming behavior to continue, yet defend against the specific accusations. Some of us strive for perfection in order to head off shame. When we are perfect, no one can find fault with us. Another shame-avoidance technique, typical in legal relationships, that is usually coupled with the quest for perfection is "winning at any cost". When we win, we cannot be shamed.

With such a mind-set, legal encounters can easily be viewed as a series of competitions, against other people and even against nature. Winning can actually consume the psyche, and any means, however nefarious, may be justified. Yet another common method for avoiding shame is to be the first to shame. When we shame others first, they can become engulfed in their own shame and cannot muster any for us. With any technique of avoiding shame comes an inability to admit mistakes or failures, much less learn from them.

Lawyers and clients can shame each other into making legal decisions which generate even more shame. Low self-esteem, denial of responsibility and obsession with winning and perfection can block our access to intuitive wisdom and can result in legal decisions inconsistent with our true desires. Shame-bound anger can escalate conflict. Lack of self-worth can perpetuate victimization. The price of winning "at any cost" can be quite high, both emotionally and financially, and can obliterate any hope of reconciliation. Relentless pursuit of perfection can lead to unrealistic legal decisions that do not account for human feelings or frailties.

When either party in a legal relationship encounters shaming behavior, the cycle of shame must be broken if the relationship is to have any chance for healthy success. Although each party is responsible for independently tracing and pulling the roots of their own shame, neither party can afford to tolerate shaming behavior from the other within the relationship. Any attempt to force consensus through shame can be immediately addressed by frankly pointing out its inappropriateness. Likewise, the strategies to be pursued with those outside the legal relationship must be thoroughly scrutinized to insure the elimination of any shaming tone. To be effective, this self-examination process should include conscious consideration of the feelings of the parties involved. Once the concept of the mind's habitual tendency to shame is understood and exposed, the parties to a legal relationship can begin to achieve more beneficial results based upon feelings which honor rather than deprecate. When a shame-free climate is achieved in our legal relationships, our intuition will have more opportunity to reveal itself, and the parties can feel better about the legal decisions that result.

Ironically, the wound caused by shame can strengthen our legal relationships when we alchemically plumb its depths to discover who we really are and what we really want. When we feel shame, we can consciously choose to mine for the intuitive gold that awaits beneath.

The Victim

Any victim demands allegiance.
—Graham Greene, English novelist, from *The Heart of the Matter*

Whining is not only graceless, but can
be dangerous. It can alert a brute that
a victim is in the neighborhood.
—Maya Angelou, American author and poet,
from *Wouldn't Take Nothing For My Journey Now*

Many lawyers see themselves as being in the business of rescuing victims, including victims of professional malpractice, automobile collisions, industrial pollution, product defects, discriminatory employers, governmental regulators and other assorted persecutors. Certainly, lawyers can provide a valuable service when victimization occurs in our society. Real victims deserve a fair opportunity to redress their grievances and an articulate spokesperson to advance their causes.

However, we have seen more and more undeserving victims, aided by colluding lawyers, abuse their access to the legal system and press for, and sometimes obtain, awards excessively disproportionate to the damage caused by their alleged victimization. Many court dockets are clogged with lawsuits of dubious merit or which involve disputes which could be better resolved extra-judiciously. Little attention within the legal system has been focused on understanding the dynamics of victimization, why it is a self-fulfilling cycle and how to help victims break the cycle by accepting more responsibility for their plight.

Lawyers receive little or no training in law school to help them prepare for the post-graduation onslaught of victims looking for rescue. I received no such training and spent many years of my law practice representing victims who would even victimize me. Many of the victims whose causes I took up would never accept any responsibility for their circumstances, and their failure to understand how they got to be a victim would inevitably doom their case. It took me a long time to figure out that every time I took the case of a person who liked being a victim and who refused to take any responsibility for their situation, I would end up investing an inordinate amount of time in a cause that would never achieve any significant measure of success. I would seldom get fully compensated for my services, and the client would usually blame me for the failure of the legal system to rescue them.

There is a dynamic in many legal relationships that is triangular in nature. The three points of the triangle can be characterized as victim, rescuer and persecutor.

The victim is the person who cries for help from another because self-help does not seem to be a viable alternative, at least from the victim's point of view. For some, this type of behavior can be comfortable and habitual and is often ingrained at an early age, usually through shame. Many victims believe that they do not have any personal power to redress wrongs or to otherwise stand up for themselves. This belief often arises because they were never taught that they have any power to act whenever they are faced with one of life's challenges. Victims generally give away their power to change their life circumstances and then blame another person or events for taking what was freely given. Victims can call attention to the atrocities of their persecutor but seldom take responsibility for their empowerment of the persecutor. Some victims enjoy the status of "victimhood" because they get comfort from rescuers. Victims often want others to comfort them, because they do not know how to take care of themselves.

Rescuers are people who believe that they can save victims.

Some rescuers believe that not only can the rescue from the immediate danger be accomplished, they can forever lift the victim out of harm's way. This unrealistic view is sometimes accompanied by the rescuer's desire to be perceived as a conquering hero, worthy of great praise and adoration. Unrealistic rescuers are usually insecure and curiously, like some victims, need psychological strokes from others. What better way to get them than to rescue a victim. The motivations of misdirected rescuers often fluctuate between the naive and the egotistic and are rarely, if ever, concerned with selfless service.

A rescuer can be a victim's worst psychological ally. When victims choose to cry foul instead of changing the behavior that surrenders their personal power, their unhealthy choice is always justified when the next rescuer in line appears. When rescuers arrive on the scene to save the day by intervening between victims and their capacity to choose from among life's circumstances, the opportunity for victims to experience the consequences of their actions and to reclaim their personal power usually vanishes.

A naive rescuer and a willing victim often relate to each other codependently. In most cases, the persecutor they align against is their collective shadow projection. It then becomes very difficult for either the rescuer or the victim to deal realistically with their projected persecutor as a human being having real feelings. In many legal relationships, there is no physical contact or personal communication between the victim and the persecutor. The rescuing lawyer often assumes the role of the communicator or the actor and will fight the persecuting dragon as the victim's knight in shining armor, while the victim is lounging back at the castle waiting for news from the front.

The persecutor is usually the person whom the victim and the rescuer both perceive to be the villain who is causing the victim to suffer distress. The persecutor can also be the ominous "they" who are always out to get the victim. "They" can be a government, a bureaucracy, an institution, a corporation or just life's inexorable circumstances.

When the rescue is not a quick success, the victim may feel betrayed by the rescuer whom the victim believes has joined the insensitive ranks of the persecutor and is actually working against the victim's best interests. Hence, to the victim, the rescuer may now become another persecutor. The victim may even persecute the former rescuer for the perceived betrayal, and the rescuer may then become the victim's victim.

Sound convoluted? It is, but this scenario typifies many lawyer-client relationships. Many clients initially enter the legal relationship as helpless victims, and many lawyers unrealistically see themselves as self-righteous rescuers. Many times they join together to combat a perceived persecutor without conscious attention to what may be the dynamics of an old pattern which, if played out again, can result in certain disappointment.

Of course, not every legal service can be characterized as a victim-rescue. Many legal undertakings are indeed noble and necessary efforts to redress real grievances and set cultural and societal standards for acceptable conduct. However, many other legal efforts are initiated by victims and rescuers who blindly act out their roles, and neither wants to take responsibility for the ensuing results.

Many of my relationships with clients have taught me the consequences of my failure to be more discriminating about whom I want to rescue and how I go about the task. Most of my lessons have been painful. In the past, when I agreed to represent clients who expected me to solve problems for them without acknowledging that they had some responsibility for the creation of the problem or, at least, for the effort necessary to resolve it, I inevitably regretted my decision. Most of these clients invariably became hypercritical of my representation, and when solutions did not quickly materialize to their satisfaction, I was easily perceived by them to be part of their problem. They usually rejected any solution that would require them to make reasonable and necessary compromises. When they self-righteously believed that they were entitled to be rescued, they often directed me to take the most litigious legal action which would, of course, result in higher legal fees that they would later decide they did not owe. Again and again, I would mount the white stallion of justice and ride off to wage war against the evil heathens only to see my client's name on my list of unpaid receivables long after the battle.

My clients would also suffer from their choice to act like a victim. Many of them could never quite understand how they came to be embroiled in a protracted legal controversy. Without an understanding of how they got involved, they could never figure out how to gracefully extricate themselves. Happy endings seemed hard to come by.

Now, when a client speaks to me of victimization, we first explore whether the client can accept responsibility for his or her legal situation and to what extent the client is willing to be responsible for fashioning a realistic and reasonable solution that empowers, not weakens. When I now get ready to ride off into the sunset, I make sure my client and I are on the same horse.

It is actually possible for client-victims to change their pattern of behavior which automatically blames someone "out there" for their plight. Lawyer-rescuers can also learn to set aside their egos long enough to refuse to participate in a futile rescue attempt and instead to help the client practice self-responsibility and self-empowerment. Working together consciously, lawyers and clients can discover new ways to break old habits.

Sex and Gender

Once sex rears its ugly 'ead it's time to steer
clear.
—Margery Allingham, English crime fiction
writer, from *Flowers for the Judge*

Nothing can inhibit the success of a legal relationship faster than gender bias or a sexual agenda. Because flirting with the opposite sex was a behavior I learned at an early age, it was very difficult for me to have a professional relationship with a woman without engaging in subtle, and sometimes overt, flirtation. I actually believed flirting was cute.

Many of my female clients did not appreciate my flirtatious behavior, and our joint legal decision-making process would often suffer because my clients would naturally have less confidence in my judgment. I could not be completely trusted because I had intruded where I was not welcome.

When women were not offended by my flirtation or even responded positively to it, my effectiveness as a lawyer was still impaired. Our mutual desire to be liked by the other usually distracted both of us from the accomplishment of the legal undertaking at hand.

Even after I became aware of my tendency to relate with female clients flirtatiously and made a conscious effort to eliminate sexual undercurrents in my professional relationships, I would still encounter some women who would perceive my friendliness as flirtation. I realized that awareness of my tendency and neutralization of its effect were not enough. I discovered that I also had to avoid any appearance of flirtation by carefully weighing how I exhibited friendliness and by immediately reacting to any sexual overtures reflected back from a client with a clear message that our relationship was to remain strictly professional, without exception.

When we enter a legal relationship, we bring our bodies with us. If we are heterosexual by nature, different dynamics are usually present when we come into contact with a person of the opposite sex than when we interact with someone of the same sex.

When we reach puberty, sexual energy takes control of our bodies. In adolescence, most of our relationships with the opposite gender are dominated by sexual feelings. We receive little or no instruction about what to do with this energy or what it is really asking us to understand about ourselves. For many of us, long after we leave adolescence, this energy has not moved out of our loins. We have no guidance to help us understand and harness this energy for our spiritual development. Many of us still confuse sexual energy with personal power. This confusion is often reflected in the marketplace. Much of our commercial advertising equates social status with sex appeal and plays to the mistaken belief that the highest use of sexual energy is its physical expression.

For numerous and complex reasons many of us reach adulthood with an immature and underdeveloped sense of our sexuality, and many of us continue to relate to the opposite gender in a sexually seductive fashion. Some of us cannot have a man-woman relationship of any kind without sexual connotations. Business conversations are often interspersed with sexual jokes and sexual innuendo. Habitual flirting is commonplace. Professional advice of any kind is often mingled with conversational sexual foreplay.

Apart from sexual interplay, many of us were taught to treat members of the opposite sex differently. Our parents and our societal role models portray certain images of how a man is supposed to relate to a woman and vice versa. Many of these images are imprinted in our subconscious mind and can result in habitual responses to the opposite sex in our legal relationships which have nothing to do with sexual impulses. For example, if a man's father dominated and controlled his mother, then the same man, now a lawyer, may unconsciously attempt to dominate and control his female client. This example also illustrates the projection of the male lawyer's image of his mother's weakness onto all women, including his female client now sitting before him, whom he can control "for her own good."

Another example might be a male lawyer who, as a child, was abandoned by his father and was left to be his mother's "little man of the house". He may project his perception of his helpless and victimized mother onto a female client and unrealistically attempt to rescue her "legally", thus impairing his objectivity and ultimately causing her harm.

A female lawyer may have had an abusive father, and she now unrealistically suspects the motives of all men. For example, she may now advise her female client to reject a reasonable compromise with a male adversary. A female client likewise may have had an abusive father and project her unresolved anger onto a male lawyer.

These simplified examples of gender bias are generally the result of projections of deeply embedded beliefs formed in our unconscious past, and it is important to be aware that such projections may be present in our professional relationships and that they can become magnified in intensity when the outcome of the legal relationship is critical to our financial survival or our emotional well-being.

Lawyers and clients can be aware of the dynamics of sexual attraction and gender bias and remain alert so these tendencies do not cloud the professional relationship. Overt and covert sexual agendas and gender confusion can easily hamper the successful realization of clients' goals and quickly ruin a lawyer's reputation.

If the lawyer-client relationship is to be true to its purpose, lawyers and clients must "steer clear" of habitual sexual behavior.

The intent to deal as human to human instead of as male to female or female to male must be mutual and conscious to be effective. Lawyers and clients can enter their relationships keenly responsible for each's own intent and can vigilantly avoid actions or language which are sexually suggestive, gender-biased or simply extraneous to a discussion about legal options.

If the other person does not acknowledge our clarity and continues to digress from the relationship's purpose, then straightforward admonishment can be appropriate, and we can learn to deliver it without fear of jeopardizing the relationship. In any event, we can be direct, refer to our feelings and ask for what we want. For example, "That language is very distracting; can we work together without it?"

If the direct approach is too stressful to attempt or our requests for change have no effect on the other person, we may risk unsatisfactory and even disastrous legal consequences if we continue the relationship.

Denial and Rationalization

I am the spirit that always denies.
—Johann Wolfgang von Goethe, from *Faust*,
'Studierzimmer'

Hence with denial vain, and coy excuse.
—John Milton, from "Lycidas"

Legal solutions which do not consider the feelings of everyone affected by them are usually inherently flawed. Even though they may work in the short term, they often ultimately unravel and may even generate the very conflict they sought to avoid.

When I deny my feelings and rationalize that they have no place in my professional life, my relationships with my clients suffer. Expression of feelings, especially those accompanied by strong emotion, was not encouraged in my family during my childhood. Consequently, I learned that it was safer to present and justify my point of view in terms of logical and linear thoughts instead of in terms of intuitive perceptions and feelings. For example, if I did not have a specific reason for saying "no", my feeling that "no" was an appropriate response for me did not get expressed.

I therefore naturally felt "at home" in the legal profession. My law school curriculum reinforced my belief that my feelings were not worth considering, much less expressing, when it came to solving legal problems. Even though my personal experience in law school included an innovative program which involved thoughtful consideration of ethical issues, no instruction was given concerning the importance of my intuition, its expression through my feelings and how to successfully access either of them in my legal relationships.

When I graduated into the world of lawyer-client relationship, I had few tools to enable me to effectively cope with the gamut of psychological and emotional situations that I would encounter. I did not know how to consciously identify my own intuitive feelings, much less those of my clients.

Over the years that followed, I learned through painful experience that my clients were increasingly demanding a deeper level of service from me. I finally surrendered to the uncharted territory of intuition and feelings, and as I clumsily embraced this unknown realm, I was amazed to find most of my clients ready and willing to participate in legal decisions that consider the feelings of everyone who are ultimately affected by them. I began to realize that before any positive change could occur in my legal relationships, I needed to stop denying my intuition and feelings and quit rationalizing legal solutions that did not take them into account.

Denial is a mental defense mechanism that is often triggered when we are asked to relate to our feelings. Because many of us have had no experience or training in how to listen to our feelings, when someone asks us how we feel, we often deny that we are feeling anything. Denial of our feelings is usually a safe answer because we then do not have to deal with them. We may be afraid to explore our feelings because we cannot logically explain them. We are afraid of "losing it", losing the safety of a logical and predictable world that usually works for us. Many of us have been taught that thinking is the only way to succeed and that no one has any respect for people who wear their hearts on their sleeves. We are told that the ability to compute, not emote, is the surest road to success.

When I deny my feelings and the validity of my intuition, my mind is usually quick to rationalize why my feelings and intuition are nothing but irrelevant blips on my screen of consciousness. When I do not honor and express my intuition and feelings, I often need facts and figures to make me feel secure, and my mind rapidly and mercifully responds.

Within the context of the lawyer-client relationship, denial and rationalization can be very destructive. When the lawyer and the client tacitly agree that their intuition and feelings have nothing to do with the solution to a legal problem, the result, although technically correct, may ultimately serve no one. When discordant feelings are ignored in the decision-making process, they can later hinder the effective implementation of the decision that is made or, at least, insure less-than-full satisfaction with it.

Denial and rationalization in lawyer-client relationships can have an impact far beyond the immediate boundaries of the professional relationship and can produce consequences that affect everyone in our society. When the law is viewed by the lawyer and client as only a mental exercise requiring cold analysis and nothing else, sensitivity for the "rightness" of the law becomes difficult to cultivate. When lawyers and clients deny their intuition and feelings, it is also easy for them to rationalize that they only have to minimally comply with the law and that they need not give any consideration to the public's best interests. This mental state can keep lawyers and clients from relating to and empathizing with the consequences of their decisions.

Decisions made by lawyers and clients can affect all of us. Some decisions have a more obvious effect than others. For example, a decision by a business and its lawyers to eliminate the polluting side effects of the business instead of just minimally complying with federal or state pollution standards would enhance the lives of all people harmed by the pollution. When decision-makers allow their feelings to connect them with the people affected by their decisions, they will often choose to honor their feelings instead of rationalizing another course of action based solely upon economics and the law's minimum standards.

A great deal of courage may be required to stop denying and rationalizing, especially when the mind has been conditioned to look for the easy way out. Some of us fiercely defend our right to resort to a purely self-serving legal action even when we know such action offends our inner sense of morality. This can change when we understand how our minds have been conditioned to deny our feelings and rationalize solutions which are devoid of any connection to our intuition. This revelation can yield legal decisions which reflect higher wisdom, not just technical perfection. Our denial can then give way to exploration of how we feel so we can benefit from our intuitive resources.

When we allow feelings such as love, compassion or even a gut-level sense of what is just or right to enter our legal decision-making processes, we can actually raise the collective consciousness of the legal profession as a whole and lead it to a higher ethical octave.

Many Voices

Do I contradict myself?
Very well then I contradict myself,
(I am large, I contain multitudes.)
  —Walt Whitman, from "Song of Myself"

From the moment I meet a prospective client and agree to perform legal services, different thoughts arise in response to what I see, hear and sense. Sometimes, certain series of thoughts suggest that I take a particular course of action or inaction, while another series of thoughts argue for a contrary course. Yet another chain of thoughts may clamor for me to chart a course somewhere in between. Some of these groups of thoughts are also charged with emotions I experienced in the past when I encountered a similar situation.

Each of these groups of thoughts seem to emanate from a place within me that has developed its own unique perspective through a lifetime of experiences. It is as if each cluster of thoughts forms the outline or pattern of a particular, and sometimes peculiar, personality trait and speaks to me with a distinctive voice.

In my early legal relationships I would usually listen to and act upon the most persistent of these recurring voices which was often the one accompanied by the most intense emotional charge. My habit of doing this would invariably complicate either my relationship with my client or my efforts to advance my client's cause.

For example, when it came to financial decisions, I would often listen to my inner accountant who would keep meticulous track of how much money my client owed me at the expense of my devotion to the legal task at hand. When it came to a client's tale of victimization at the hands of government or big business, my naive hero would usually join forces with my angry rebel to wage a costly legal battle only to discover that my client was partly or wholly responsible for his or her situation. When I was faced with unfamiliar or threatening legal territory, I would sometimes listen to my inner coward who would then convince my client to select another course of action from my safer, albeit limited, legal repertoire.

When we listen closely, we can hear many internal characters who voice various opinions concerning our daily decisions. Sometimes it is our inner warrior, sometimes our playful, innocent or hurt child, sometimes our naive adult, sometimes our old man or old woman, sometimes our shadow, sometimes nature, sometimes anger or sometimes fear, envy or jealousy. The strongest voice or voices usually get their way, and our lives unfold accordingly. If the resulting course and quality of our lives and our legal decisions leaves something to be desired, then we can begin to identify our inner characters and learn how to deal with them more effectively.

I am using the metaphor of separate and distinct inner characters to describe psychological archetypes and emotional qualities that most of us can relate to. Carl Jung defined archetypes as mythological components common to us collectively. June Singer, in her book *Boundaries of the Soul: The Practice of Jung's Psychology*, explains that archetypes represent "certain regularities, consistently recurring types of situations and types of figures." Joseph Campbell has also contributed an important body of work to this subject. Here, I am also including in our cast of inner characters any strong emotion that seems to repeatedly direct our behavior.

The suggestion of this book is to follow our heart's intuition as revealed by our feelings, but which feelings do we follow? And how do we distinguish our feelings from the many voices of our mind?

The internal voices which shape our lives have a combination of origins. Some are developed in childhood as our view of the world is being shaped by our environment, others are common to the particular culture in which we are born, and many are archetypal, intrinsic to human evolution on this planet.

When we are in relationship, all of these voices have something to say. The extent to which we give each of them weight determines the course of our personal experience. It is as if we each carry within us a story involving this inner cast of characters, and the plot and ending of any particular relationship, including a legal relationship, is usually dependent upon which of these characters are allowed to assume starring, supporting or background roles. The reason the word "allowed" is used is intentional. Each of these characters has the capacity to assume command of our inner stage on their own and can automatically take command over and over again unless we make a conscious effort to understand them and do the casting ourselves.

We see out-of-control casting in most legal relationships. For example, the client's anger can join forces with the lawyer's naive adult, or the client's victim can take the stage with the lawyer's rescuer. Whatever the combination, such unconscious casting can produce an undesirable ending.

On a macrocosmic scale, the injury resulting from inept character casting can harm the planet itself. For example, when our innate interconnectedness with nature is relegated to a background role, the earth is usually in immediate danger. Because of the fundamental role lawyers and laws play in determining the quality of our life on the planet, a disregard of the voice of nature can inevitably injure our physical environment as well as the people who live within it. When we ignore the voice of nature, we are vulnerable to our voices that can rationalize long-term damage to the ecological balance in exchange for short-term profit.

True integration of our "self" in a legal relationship seems to demand that we acknowledge all of the actors available to participate in our legal decision-making process but learn how to assign roles to them that can best result in the ending that we desire. Such cast selection requires us to be conscious of who within our psyches is available to participate. Conscious cast selection also requires the development of an ability to dialogue with our more powerful and potentially destructive tendencies in order to help them accept appropriate supporting or background roles.

Once we identify and understand all of the voices or tendencies of our mind, our plot and actor selection can then be guided by our feelings, which are not intellectually directed. By getting in touch with what feels right for us, we can effect a positive change of our legal scripts, and our minds and hearts can begin to co-create healthier legal relationships with happier endings.

The Corporate Mind

Corporations have neither bodies to be
punished, nor souls to be condemned,
they therefore do as they like.
— 1st Baron Thurlow Edward, English jurist,
from John Poynder, *Literary Extracts*

I have represented many corporations and with very few excep-
tions, the larger the corporation, in terms of number of stockholders and employees, the more removed the managers and
owners are from feeling directly responsible for the actions of
the corporation.

Early in my business law practice, I helped incorporate a business owned and operated by a father and his sons by blood and
marriage. The business had started out in the father's garage, and
in a relatively short period of time, its annual revenues exceeded
a million dollars. Their accountant told them they should incorporate for tax reasons, and they came to me for assistance.

I carefully explained to them that we were creating a separate
legal entity and that we had to issue stock to the father, sons and
sons-in-law. I told them that they needed to vote their stock for
a board of directors who would, in turn, elect officers to operate the business. I advised them that they needed to provide for
the future disposition of their stock in the event one of them died,
went bankrupt, was disabled or left the business. During the time
that I represented them, their business continued to grow and
flourish. Two new corporations were created, and more stock
was divided up among the family members.

Over the course of the four years that I represented these corporations, I began to notice flaws in my creation. As the family
members became more sophisticated about how to wield power

within the corporation by voting blocks of stock, they became less concerned about their joint enterprise and their allegiance to their family and more concerned about protecting their individual interests. Some favored rapid expansion of the business while others missed the camaraderie of the pre-incorporation family unit and wanted the business to operate on a smaller scale. Board and stockholder meetings became more and more formal, and there was little discussion of how everyone felt about the changes in their family relationships brought on by the sudden growth of the business.

Finally, several members of the family withdrew from the corporations at a great financial cost to the business and to the remaining stockholders. Their withdrawal dealt a traumatic blow to already deteriorating intra-family relations, and it was accomplished with a cruel emotional detachment.

I had been an inside observer over the years, and I knew that the family was coping with dynamics that are common to rapid wealth and success. Yet, I also felt that the family's demise was significantly accelerated when they began to relate to each other through corporate structures which seemed to distance them from how they felt about the expansion of their business and how it was affecting their relationships with each other. I came away from that experience much more motivated to advise clients of the need to continue to voice their feelings after incorporating their business, so that they would not become isolated by their new corporate identity and shirk responsibility for the effect their corporate actions would inevitably have on others.

The corporation is a relatively recent addition to our culture's legal landscape. Its appearance on the scene coincided with the industrialization of society and the consequent separation of people from their families and from their land.

The economic reasoning was sound: interchangeable parts and assembly-line production are more efficient than cottage diversification. However, the psychological aftermath was less-than-desirable. As people were drawn to the cities to participate in the American dream, the family structure that had traditionally provided psychological stability yielded to a business hierarchy that was less durable and less nurturing. The "organization" became the surrogate psychological head of the family.

This transition in our collective consciousness was mirrored in our legal system by the recognition of the corporation as a legal fiction, separate and equal under the law with rights and duties identical to those of the individual.

As the size of industries and their need for large amounts of capital outgrew the ability of our traditional legal structures to accommodate them, the corporation was heralded as the answer. In the latter part of the 19th century, the corporation was legally recognized as a business entity of indefinite duration owned by shareholders who could come and go at will.

The corporation was legally charged with assuming human responsibility for the collective action of an amorphous group of people. A "thing" was bestowed with the power to affect humans and their physical environment without any direct human accountability. In the commercial world, personal commitment of one's self to another human became more of a concept than a reality.

The handshake used to symbolize personal commitment. When two people "shook on it", it was a serious event invoking an acceptance of personal responsibility for the accomplishment of a mutually agreed undertaking. Now, "corporate" handshakes have less solemn meaning. The shakers do not have to commit themselves personally to each other because they are representing corporations, which have logos for faces.

This lack of personal commitment to the fulfillment of an agreement removes the psyche a critical step away from responsibility for the final outcome. The mind welcomes and rationalizes this separation, since accepting personal responsibility is often perceived to be a stressful obligation. It is safer and easier to agree to a less-than-responsible corporate course of action when the corporation's failure to perform responsibly cannot be easily traced to any particular individual.

The corporate mind is characterized by abstract thought and anonymity, abstract because there is usually no direct individual connection with a physical reality and anonymous because there is often no direct responsibility to the people interacting with the corporation.

The natural tendency of the corporate mind is to disconnect thoughts and actions from intuition and feelings. As long as no individual human being bears responsibility for the ultimate corporate act, human feelings about the consequences of the act are easier to discount or avoid. Lawyers naturally contribute to this disconnection when they insulate their clients from personal liability with corporate shields and thereby distance them from individual responsibility.

Many clients are attracted to the idea of reducing their personal exposure to financial loss, so they eagerly incorporate upon the advice of their counsel. Decision-making then focuses on "corporate" considerations, and the human feelings associated with the consequences of the decisions generally take a back seat to the bottom line. And so it goes.

The mind-set that pervades our corporate culture often has little feeling for the consequences of the acts of the corporate body. This abdication can occur within any large group, but the corporation's organizational distinction between owners and operators unwittingly severs its feeling body from its rational head, denying the corporation both the benefit and the responsibility of human feelings and compassion. Because corporate decision-makers can easily insulate themselves from personal responsibility for their decisions, corporate decision-making can become correspondingly more short-sighted than it would be if there were direct individual accountability to those affected by corporate decisions.

Because the mammoth corporations of today can wield more

power than governments, conscious legal decision-making at the corporate level may be crucial to our survival as a people. It is within the realm of possibility for lawyers and business people to be reconnected to their intuitive and feeling natures and weigh corporate decisions accordingly. Even though the reintroduction of a consideration of intuition and feelings into the corporate process may not turn a quick profit, it can help sustain the corporate body over the long haul by connecting the movers and the shakers with the feelings of those being moved and shaken.

New forums that encourage heartfelt feedback from directors, officers, shareholders and employees concerning the effect of corporate policies are needed. Lawyers can be trained to solicit underlying feelings from the officers, directors and shareholders of their corporate clients about prospective decisions, to facilitate intuitive decision-making and to advise against and refuse to participate in decisions which simply do not feel right. When the consideration of feelings and intuition is made a priority by those who make legal decisions for corporations, we may find that corporations can act compassionately toward those people who are directly affected by the exercise of corporate power and still enjoy financial success.

The bridging of the gap between decisions made in an economic vacuum and empathy for the ultimate effect on people and the planet must begin with an understanding of how the corporate mind affects each relationship within the corporate structure. When people within the corporate system are encouraged to make conscious choices between group conformity and personal integrity, the corporate mind can be balanced and even enhanced by the feeling heart.

Competition

For when the One Great Scorer comes to
mark against your name,
He writes-not that you won or lost-but
how you played the Game.
　—Grantland Rice, American sports writer,
　　from "Alumnus Football"

I have competed all my life, against others and against myself. Competition was deeply instilled in me at a very young age. I learned to compete for affection and for attention. I learned that winning was more rewarding than losing. When I was introduced to the world of competitive sports, I also learned that winning was even more rewarding than playing the game. Law school only reinforced my conviction that winning was everything. Even as a lawyer, I was obsessed with victory, and I took my losses very hard. I chose to represent almost every client that came to me as if they were engaged in some form of competitive battle, pitted against someone or something. I constantly evaluated my performance as a lawyer in terms of how many cases I "won" or "lost".

I would not have re-evaluated my competitive approach to my profession when I did were it not for my children and step-children. As they reached the age when they could play adult board and card games, they would challenge me to play with them. I played these games with my usual competitive vigor, and within a short period of time, none of the children wanted to play with me. My mental intensity, rigid obsession with rules and need to win took the fun out of virtually every game we played.

It was through this painful process that I finally began to comprehend that my competitive drive was also responsible for creating an unhealthy climate in many of my legal relationships and that there was more to my professional life than winning. I realized that I was pushing many of my clients to make aggressive legal decisions which were not always in their best interests.

It began to dawn on me that many legal situations could be successfully resolved without competition when I enabled ostensible adversaries to join together in pursuit of their common interests and when I encouraged my clients to accept more responsibility for the consequences of their actions. When I began to better understand my addiction to competition, the results of my legal efforts were no longer limited to either absolute victory or abject defeat. I discovered that a vast new world lay between the two extremes and that non-competitive opportunities were indeed available to me and, more importantly, to my clients.

"Compete" is derived from the Latin "competere" which means "to come together or to coincide". However, most of us do not associate competition with this derivation. We are more familiar with the modern definition, "to vie for the same object, to be put in rivalry with." It is in this latter sense that our mind usually functions. Most of us are trained at an early age to find differences between objects and people, and the more distinctions we can make, the more intelligent we are believed to be.

It is little wonder that the word "competition" characterizes our society's legal process. It is also no coincidence that the caption of every lawsuit includes the word "versus".

When we enter the legal arena, we bring with us every competitive experience of our life, from Little League baseball to climbing the corporate ladder, from sibling rivalry to school rivalry, from competing for love and affection to constantly measuring our appearance and performance against our inner ideal of who we should be. Our mind ceaselessly compares us with ourself and with others and often reasons that differences between similar objects or people mean that something or someone has to be better than another thing or someone else. The purpose of these comparisons is usually to determine who wins and who loses, who is superior to and who is not as good as.

Legal counseling therefore is often comparable to a discussion of move selection in a chess game. One player is pitted against the other. The goal is to outmaneuver and defeat the opponent, whether the opponent be another person, a business or the government.

Any competition, including legal competition, also has its price. There must be a loser. Someone must be designated as not as good as someone else. We all know the pain of this experience, of being labeled a loser. Every winner has been a loser, and even in winning, we are reminded of the pain of losing when we look into the loser's eyes. Because our mind is capable of denying our feelings of compassion and rationalizing that they are irrelevant, it is easy to distance ourself from the memory of our experience of losing by simply depersonalizing the competition. For example, we can insure that we do not have to relate to a loser's pain when we secure our win by dropping "smart" bombs on a distant enemy whom we describe in inhuman, impersonal terms, such as the "enemy" or the "defendants". It is difficult to have compassion for suffering that we keep at a distance.

Competition is often based upon fear, fear that losing means loneliness, incompleteness or loss of identity. When we compete with another, our competition can also be a sign of our insecurity, for if we were secure in our knowledge of who we are, why would we have to prove it to anyone?

In our culture, most of us have been conditioned to believe that certain positive character traits and useful life tools can only be developed through competition. Many of us are told that it is helpful for us to know how to win and lose gracefully, that our experiences in the "school of hard knocks" will make us more likely to succeed in life. Indeed, many of us rely on competition to push us beyond our self-limitations.

The down side of competition is seldom discussed. Many of

us never realize that our obsession with winning can keep the real success that is born of compassion and reconciliation always just out of reach. We rarely consider what life without competition can be like.

We also are not taught the fine line between competition in sports and competition in life and when we should not mix the two. Many of us believe that the "thrill of victory and the agony of defeat" are the only available outcomes in virtually every life situation. Not only do many of us see life as a series of competitive struggles, but we also expect that a decisive result should be achieved within the time it takes to conduct a sporting event. When a quick resolution does not occur, we can become frustrated, confused and angry.

The same holds true for legal relationships where winning and losing are touted as the only prospects. So long as the focus of the relationship is only on winning, the outcome runs a high risk of being unsatisfactory or incomplete.

When we openly acknowledge our mind's predisposition to compete and refuse to allow competition to determine the course of our legal relationships, we can begin to create a matrix of non-competitive alternatives that will accommodate legal solutions which are specifically designed to benefit all parties involved. When we make this breakthrough in consciousness, we can allow our intuition and our feelings to guide us to legal decisions that provide a space and context in which all parties can co-exist without conflict and without humiliation. Such a decision-making process will usually entail the recognition, not comparison, of the differences of the parties as pieces of a larger puzzle, instead of as separate interests competing for a single role. Our differences can then "come together, or coincide," as the Latin definition of "compete" intended.

When we discover new ways for our differences to peacefully co-exist, we can concentrate on working together instead of in opposition. Such legal solutions are almost always win-win.

Many models for such a shift in perspective have been proposed. One of the best discussions of what it takes to make this paradigm transition can be found in *The Seven Habits of Highly Effective People* by Stephen Covey.

Legal decision-making and the legal system as a whole can also benefit enormously from the introduction of less competitive techniques of problem solving and dispute resolution such as informal arbitration and mediation. However, unless we dig up the roots of our desire to compete, such forums are only band-aid solutions applied to a hemorrhaging legal process. What the patient really needs is a complete infusion of a new consciousness that specifically intends to eliminate the competitive dynamic from legal relationships altogether. Instead of competing with each other in negotiation, arbitration, mediation or in court, we can learn how *not* to compete at all within and through each of our legal relationships. The cultivation of non-competitive attitudes through formal training programs established within the legal system can help us finally acknowledge that win-win, not win-lose, will ensure the best results for clients facing virtually any legal challenge.

The Hero Warrior

ANDREA: Unhappy the land that has no
  heroes!...
GALILEI: No. Unhappy the land that needs
  heroes.
  —Bertolt Brecht, German playwright, from
  "Leben des Galilei"

America's present need is not heroics, but
  healing...
  —President Warren G. Harding, from a speech
  given in Boston, May 14, 1920

Doctors...still retain a high degree of
public confidence because they are perceived
as healers. Should lawyers not be healers?
Healers, not warriors? Healers, not procurers?
Healers, not hired guns?
  —Supreme Court Justice Warren E. Burger, to
  American Bar Association, February 12,
  1984

I was born in 1947, two years after the end of World War II,
when Americans saw themselves as heroes and warriors, invin-
cible yet chivalrous, the designated enforcers of truth and justice in the modern world. During my first twenty years of life,
my success seemed to depend upon how well I measured up to
this distinctly American version of the perfect man.

The war in Vietnam was a critical turning point for me. As
America's institutions broke apart upon the rocks of lies and
injustice, I became disenchanted with our cultural archetype of
the hero and actually rebelled against it. Although there was
ample justification for my disillusionment, I would not begin to
replace what I had rejected with anything substantial until another
twenty years had passed. In fact, I continued to measure my suc-

cess in life against the pre-Vietnam cultural standard because it was so ingrained in my psyche. Even though I had shifted intellectually, my personal and professional life still suffered from the effects of my macho shadow. As a lawyer, I was aggressive and competitive and would easily lose sight of the big picture in my effort to heroically find a legal technicality or "loophole" that would enable my clients to avoid responsibility for their actions. I would ignore my intuition concerning the rightness or wrongness of what I was doing, and I would make little or no effort to elicit my clients' feelings about the legal services I was providing.

Unfortunately, I achieved just enough success to avoid having to search for a better way to practice my profession. Fortunately, I had married a woman who would not tolerate my lack of attention to my feelings. As my personal struggle to create healthier family relationships progressed, I also began to see my relationships with my clients in a different light.

I slowly began to reconnect with those sensitive parts of me that I had buried in childhood because I had been taught that they were not useful to an American hero warrior. As I changed, so did my relationships with my clients. I discovered that my legal relationships became more successful when my clients and I would communicate our feelings and trust our intuition. I am also discovering that I am not alone, as the American perception of the lawyer as a hero warrior appears to be undergoing intense reexamination by many people in our society.

The establishment of America as a powerful industrialized country was accomplished by pioneering personalities who usually "conquered" any challenge they would face by aggressively exercising physical and/or intellectual strength. The modern American hero has traditionally been the "man" who "aggressively" "advances" "upward" through a "hierarchy" by "beating" his "competitors". He is "decisive", "logical" and has a strong "will". The legal profession has naturally adopted this model for achieving success that may well have played a useful role during our country's early years.

However, there are now cracks in this historical bulwark that are becoming increasingly apparent. The American version of the lawyer as a hero warrior is now in crisis. We are realizing that our legal "man" comes replete with a steamer trunk full of shadow material. He is frequently unbalanced, and his psychological dysfunctioning is more evident than ever.

The industrial world he has helped create is losing touch with the earth it sits on. With his hierarchical and rational thinking has come a rigidity that cannot easily adapt to necessary change. His competitiveness has deteriorated into a destructive fascination with power and winning, regardless of the cost. With his defense of technology has come a disconnection from family and nature, which has resulted in widespread emotional stress and loss of sense of purpose.

Our culture's unhealthy version of the legal hero warrior parallels the "dis-ease" that exists between male and female, not only between men and women but also between "male" characteristics within women and "female" characteristics within men. When I use the terms "male" and "female" in this context, I am referring to psychological archetypes, not generic characteristics of men and women. Both archetypes are present in all men and in all women, and the degree to which they manifest varies with each individual, regardless of gender.

"Male characteristics" are those tendencies toward outward-directed or active behavior, primarily concerned with controlling or stabilizing the physical environment. Words which describe the psychological import of the term "male" are order, power, authority, structure, rigidity, aggression, initiation, domination, "I think", analytical, logical, scientific, definite, will, judgment, rational, mind.

The opposite of the embodiment of these tendencies is characterized as "female", described by words such as unknown, receptive, "I feel", nurturing, creative, mysterious, intuitive, yielding, compassionate, sensitive, changeable, flexible, forgiveness, vague, nature, heart. These terms describe personal attributes that are inward-directed and sensitive to the well-being of the immediate environment.

As I indicated, "male" and "female" describe psychological tendencies and are not intended to delineate men and women. However, we naturally experience an urge to assign the "male" tendencies to men and the "female" tendencies to women, as our culture has taught us that men should display male and avoid female characteristics and women should display female and avoid male characteristics.

The health of our legal system depends upon the extent to which we can balance both male and female characteristics in ourselves and in our professional relationships. It is indeed possible to be both aggressive and yielding, rigid and flexible, logical and intuitive, initiatory and receptive, scientific and mysterious, powerful and nurturing, analytical and compassionate, thinking and feeling. These apparently opposing attributes are not really opposite at all and can paradoxically exist simultaneously.

Young men and women, whose upbringing emphasized allegiance to the American hero warrior archetype, whose childhoods were full of parental admonitions to "win" and "achieve", are naturally drawn to a legal profession that "goes by the book" and plays abstract, unfeeling mind and word games to determine a legal "winner". It is ironic that as more men and women in our society are now mourning their lost "female" and "male" selves, the legal system appears to be getting more rigid and is generating even more lawyer jokes.

Law schools offer very little, if any, training in understanding how humans relate, how the mind works, how important feelings and intuition are, yet lawyers graduate from law school into a population "in relationship" and find that most of their legal work is about relationships. Lawyers, who have no relationship training and who are generally drawn to the profession because they are out of touch with their own feelings, are being asked to help their clients deal with challenges based upon underlying feelings that even the clients cannot easily access. An enigma within a riddle.

Both clients and lawyers can begin to correlate this cultural context with their professional encounters and legal decisions. The American hero-warrior archetype must now be exposed for what it isn't. Male can be reunited with female. Mind can be reconnected to intuition and to feelings. When we strive to become more conscious about what unconsciously motivates us and acknowledge the value of our intuition and feelings, we can make our legal decisions, and the impact of our legal decisions upon our lives, more vibrant and more sustaining.

2

Taking Responsibility

The chess-board is the world; the pieces are
the phenomena of the universe; the rules of
the game are what we call the laws of Nature.
The player on the other side is hidden from
us. We know that his play is always fair,
just, and patient. But also we know, to our
cost, that he never overlooks a mistake, or
makes the smallest allowance for ignorance.
  —T.H. Huxley, English biologist, "A Liberal
    Education", from *Lay Sermons, Addresses,
    and Reviews*

Man's task is to become conscious of the
contents that press upward from the
  unconscious.
  —Carl Jung, from *Memories, Dreams and
    Reflections*

The blame is his who chooses...
  —Plato, from *The Republic*

More than a few clients have related their stories to me replete
with words, looks and gestures that presume that we have entered
into an unspoken conspiracy to find the easiest way out of their
legal challenge, to take them off the hook, to lighten their load,
to find the perfect loophole. Even though they may not be able
to admit it, many people want a lawyer to do whatever is necessary, ethical or otherwise, when they are in a legal pinch. Many
lawyers willingly oblige because it may be more economical for
them to justify a shaky legal position to a judge than to refuse
to participate in the unspoken conspiracy and lose a fee-

paying client.

I was trained in law school to thread the legal needle by advancing my client's interests to the outer limits of the law's envelope. When my answers to exam questions creatively probed these limits, I usually received high marks. There is no question that the law needs dynamic change, and for this to occur, limits often have to be pushed. Many lawyers, however, are more concerned with helping their clients avoid legal and moral responsibility for their actions than they are with exploring innovative legal solutions that preserve their clients' integrity. This inclination is natural in a profession that relies heavily on the ability of the mind to provide answers that do not necessarily have to feel right.

Even though we have reviewed only a few of the ways our mind functions in legal relationships, an instructive theme has begun to emerge. Our mind tends to imagine that it has no responsibility for the creation of whatever scene it is observing. What is out there is separate from what is in here.

When this tendency is allowed to direct our legal decision-making, the failures of our legal relationships will also tend to repeat themselves, and our habit of blaming others for this cyclic occurrence will sound increasingly hollow.

Our mind generally observes only what it has been trained to see. The detail of the observation is directly proportionate to the conscious capacity of our mind to observe in detail. Habitually overlooked details can repetitively result in a misdiagnosis of the nature of the object observed. For example, if a client has been conditioned to believe that authority figures are always untrustworthy and manipulative, then the client will be likely to conclude that he or she will be victimized by any authority figure with whom they come in contact. Even though this perception may not be true in the absolute, it may become absolutely true in the client's relationship with an authority figure because the perception itself is creating the reality of the client's victimization.

When a lawyer perceives that a client needs rescuing because the lawyer was conditioned at an early age to believe that heroic rescue is what everyone who asks for help needs, the reality of a victimization requiring rescue will predictably unfold.

When corporate lawyers and the board members of the corporations they represent believe that intuition and feelings are not relevant components of legal strategies because they were led to believe that the expression of their feelings would only impede their advancement in a culture which measures success by intellectual achievement, their legal decisions, even though easily justified by the rational mind, may create an actual reality which can be toxic to the human condition and can manifest itself as stress in people and as destructive pollution in the environment.

Once we understand all of the ways our predisposed mind can create less-than-desirable relationships, we can begin to assume individual responsibility for everything that flows from our legal decisions. Only then can we hope to create more positive and more successful legal relationships.

If we want our legal relationships to yield more beneficial results, we must take responsibility for the mental perceptions we carry into our relationships and understand that there is a direct connection between our perceptual approach to each legal relationship and its ultimate success.

Clients and lawyers must also pause in their blame of each other for unsatisfactory endings to their relationships and begin to examine their own mental predispositions that inevitably lead to unwise decisions. The client can review why a particular lawyer was chosen, why questions about the lawyer's work and billing were not asked, why the client deferred to the lawyer's judgment, why anger, fear, envy, sexual feelings or gender bias were allowed to cloud the client's judgment, why the client agreed to a course of action that did not totally feel right and so on. The lawyer can also ask himself or herself what motivated the acceptance of a particular case, why the client's intentions and goals were not explored in more detail, why the lawyer decided to rescue the client, why the lawyer deferred to the client's anger, fear, greed and so forth.

Instead of blaming the lawyer for an undesirable outcome, the client can take responsibility for having given the lawyer broad, non-specific authority to act on the client's behalf. Instead of blaming the client for an unsuccessful or acrimonious relationship, the lawyer can take responsibility for unwisely acceding to the client's desires or agreeing to represent the client in the first place.

Unsuccessful legal relationships do not happen by accident. They are created step by little step. They may seem like they are just one of life's random unpleasant experiences if the parties to the relationship are not consciously aware of the significance of each step of the process and how reality follows the mind's perception of it.

Once we begin to tune in to our intuition and feelings, we have to learn how to describe what we have tuned into. In our culture, the expression of an intuitive insight or a feeling that cannot be factually explained by the rational mind is not easily accepted by most of the general populace.

Our "response ability" not only depends upon our ability to locate our feeling and intuitive center; it also depends upon our ability to respond to our feelings and intuitive flashes by expressing and acting upon them. The health of our legal system can be improved by the open consideration of intuition and feelings as intrinsic parts of the legal decision-making process.

Lawyers and clients have some generic challenges to overcome if their mutual decisions are to reflect a healthy balance between the mind and the heart. Many clients are emotionally charged when they seek advice from lawyers and relate to the lawyer from a confused mixture of mental projections, emotions and feelings. Lawyers as a group tend to be less in touch with their feelings and more centered in their logical minds and therefore find it difficult to help a client access the feelings necessary for responsible decision-making.

Fundamental and lasting transformation can occur in legal relationships, and consequently in the legal system, if lawyers and clients can each take responsibility for their own psychological baggage and begin to relate consciously through their intuition and feelings. When we acknowledge that we are totally responsible for every consequence, however remote, of each legal decision we make, we no longer have to concern ourselves with the mind's efforts to lead us elsewhere. We will have arrived in that immutable space where the heart dwells and have only to await its direction.

3

Entering the Lawyer-Client Relationship

Great minds have purposes, others have wishes.
—Washington Irving

Clarifying Intent

The success of a lawyer-client relationship is dependent, in large part, upon the degree to which the lawyer and the client can achieve a clear and mutual intent. The specific purpose of the relationship should be an express provision of the contract to perform legal services. Clients engage the services of lawyers for a myriad of reasons, but only a few inclusive categories will be addressed here: dispute resolution, agreement formation and technical compliance.

Disputes

> Yea, even amongst wiser militants, how many wounds have been given, and credits slain, for the poor victory of an opinion, or the beggarly conquest of a distinction!
> —Sir Thomas Browne, English writer and physician, from *Religio Medici*

Lawyer-client relationships meet their most challenging tests in the areas of dispute resolution. When the client initially contemplates using the services of a lawyer to resolve a dispute, the dispute is usually well underway, and strong emotions have already surfaced.

For many people, the decision to employ a lawyer signifies a desire to end a dispute. Some come to a lawyer because they lack the relationship skills to deal with their own disputes. Some come because they generally perceive themselves as victims, and they want a legal rescue. Some are driven by anger and actually want to escalate the dispute. Often a combination of these reasons, all of which may not be conscious, brings clients to seek advice from a lawyer.

In law school and beyond, lawyers receive little or no training about how to help clients resolve disputes from other than a strictly legal perspective. Many lawyers are deplorably lacking in the relationship skills necessary to help their clients explore the feelings that underlie the superficial legal context of the dispute. In recent times, as the public has become more psychologically sophisticated, more clients are realizing that their lawyers are not fully equipped to facilitate decisions that serve the clients' best personal interests as well as their best legal interests. Knowing in advance that lawyers are not trained counselors may motivate some clients to be more realistic about what they hope to achieve through the legal system and to more carefully define their intentions, legal and non-legal.

Many clients are not able to articulate exactly what they want a lawyer to do for them until they come to terms with their emotions, such as hurt or anger, that want to lash out at the offender. When the voices of their emotions are consciously acknowledged, most clients can then begin to ascertain what their underlying goals are.

One way to use the process of articulation to clarify intent is for the client to write a detailed summary of what the dispute is about, how the client believes the dispute began, which aspects of the dispute are legal in nature and which are non-legal, exactly what does the client believe a lawyer can do to help resolve the dispute and why the dispute cannot be resolved without resorting to the services of a lawyer. The summary can also include a description of the emotions surrounding the dispute and how the client feels about resolving the dispute through legal means.

The prospective client may find it useful to write the prefacing words "I feel" when answering these questions in order to help the client accept responsibility for what the client intends to accomplish by legal resolution of the dispute. Otherwise, the client may be satisfied with a course of action that is nothing more than a knee-jerk reaction to the offensive behavior of the other person. Legal resolution of the dispute is more likely to succeed when the client's intent is proactive, not reactive.

When the client describes how the dispute began, it is important to reflect on the inception of the relationship with the so-called "adverse" party and to recall the first warning sign which alerted the client that the relationship with the other person might ultimately have problems. This warning sign may have been something the other person said or did or may simply have been a feeling that "told" the client that something was "off" or uncomfortable.

After that first feeling of discomfort is identified, the client can then review why the feeling was discounted or ignored and what action (or inaction) the client could have initially taken to avoid the dispute which has now led to the consideration of legal action. In other words, if the client can accept only a small part of the responsibility for his or her current predicament, non-legal solutions or, at least, less aggressive legal solutions may become more appropriate.

Lawyers can assist their clients in their efforts to clarify intent by eliciting their clients' feelings about the dispute and about their perceived adversary. Lawyers can also encourage their clients to accept at least some responsibility for their participation in and escalation of the dispute in order to help them determine the best course of action (or inaction).

It may also be useful for clients to assume full and complete responsibility for their role in the precipitation of the dispute. For example, if clients can realize that they actually invited a dispute by allowing themselves to be victimized and are still playing the role of victim by seeking rescue from a lawyer, they can begin to entertain non-legal solutions that can save them both time and expense. If they remain in denial, the issues confronting them will only temporarily divert their attention from the unconscious patterns of mental perception and behavior that make their "victimhood" a self-fulfilling prophecy.

When clients carefully acknowledge their self-defeating propensities, any necessary legal services can then be directed toward achievement of a positive and practical result rather than deteriorate into a lengthy and costly rescue from a perceived persecutor. If, after full consideration, a legal solution is still appropriate, the intent of the legal relationship can be to undertake the step-by-step reconstruction of personal and legal boundaries instead of the precipitous planning of a legal *Blitzkrieg*.

Lawyers can also refrain from making remarks or giving advice which will exacerbate the dispute. It is easier for clients to discern their true intent without pressure from their lawyer to pursue a confrontive legal remedy. Lawyers can instead remain open to the possibility of a more beneficial non-legal approach, even if it means the client may decide to resolve the dispute without the lawyer's help.

Stephen Covey's suggestion of "win-win or no deal" may also help prospective clients clarify their intent regarding resolution of a dispute. Covey suggests that in negotiating a business deal, great benefit can be gained by approaching the negotiation with the attitude that if an agreement cannot be negotiated which will clearly benefit both parties in all respects, then there should be no relationship at all between the parties, in other words, either win-win or no deal.

When a dispute is in progress, it is often difficult to encourage the disputants to explore win-win solutions because of the intensity of the emotions that can block the parties' intuitive access to win-win results. However, if the client can begin to focus on what a win-win resolution would look like and what kind of intent the client has to have to achieve it, the process of clarifying intent may actually set the stage for the successful settlement of the dispute.

When the client can accept full responsibility for his or her role in the creation and/or escalation of the dispute, the win-win or no deal approach can be even more effective. As the client accepts more responsibility for the behavior that led the client to the lawyer's office for help, the client may become less attached to winning the dispute. As the client begins to evaluate the lesson of the dispute in the larger context of life's classroom, the importance of the dispute and of winning it may diminish, and the client may even begin to experience compassion for the adverse party. When this occurs and a win-win resolution still cannot be achieved, the client may be better able to say "no deal". In other words, if both parties cannot win, the client may choose to decide that there will be no fight, no competition. In some situations, it may indeed be in the client's best interests to walk away from the dispute and chalk up the "loss" to experience.

When attempting to clarify their intent toward disputes, most lawyers and clients may not be able to immediately reverse deeply embedded psychological tendencies, and I am by no means suggesting that all unconscious obstructions to the successful resolution of legal disputes can be rooted out by simply reading this book. These things take time and may even require professional help. However, I am suggesting that open discussion of these issues may benefit any legal relationship that seeks to resolve a dispute successfully.

Agreements

> The difficulty about a gentleman's agreement is
> that it depends on the continued existence of
> gentlemen.
> —Reginald Withers Payne, Judge of the High
> Court, quoted in the *New York Times*,
> February 9, 1964

> A verbal contract isn't worth the paper it is
> written on.
> —Sam Goldwyn, American film producer,
> from *The Great Goldwyn* by Alva Johnston

When we seek legal assistance to formalize an agreement with another person, our long-term satisfaction with the final result usually depends upon our ability to articulate our true intentions and to ascertain the true intentions of the other party.

As with a dispute, we want to identify our real intent and the underlying emotions which motivate our desire to reach an agreement with the other person. The honesty necessary to accomplish this is more than just intellectual honesty which relies upon rationalization. Rather, it is the honesty which is connected to our intuition and confirmed by our feelings. It is honesty undiminished by tact or our fear of another's opinion. It is honesty which is sometimes crude and raw and is the direct product of our "gut" feeling. It is often our first physical reaction or our initial thought.

We can direct this kind of honesty inwardly as well as outwardly. Inwardly, we can admit and accept our basic motivations for pursuing an agreement, even if they could be perceived by others to be crass or selfish. If our motivations include need or even greed, it is better to acknowledge their presence so that we can then ask ourself some critical questions. Do I really want to enter into an agreement out of need? Will my immediate need cause me to impetuously make concessions which I may regret in the long run? What do I really need from this agreement for it to work for me now and in the future?

When we negotiate an agreement, it is okay for us to be selfish. No one else will be selfish for us. When we finally admit what we selfishly want out of an agreement, we can better articulate and achieve our real needs, or we may decide that an agreement with this particular person cannot ultimately give us what we want and therefore is not right for us.

We can also examine what it is that we are willing to give to the agreement. In what ways are we willing to commit our time, energy and resources to the success or performance of the agreement? Will we be naively overextending ourselves so that disharmony among the parties or even complete failure of the agreement is inevitable? Are we soliciting the agreement only because we need to secure the approval of the other party or because we are otherwise psychologically or financially dependent upon a relationship with the other party? By consciously reflecting on the nature of our commitment, we can insure that our agreement is by choice and not by habit.

Identification of what we are giving to the agreement and why can also help us to set personal boundaries which will enable us to continue to perform our part of the agreement without feeling resentment about our commitment and ultimately looking for an escape route. In other words, by deciding exactly what we are willing to do when we agree, we can also make sure that we clearly establish what we are unwilling to do.

Failure to be scrupulously honest with ourselves during this process can cloud our judgment and can result in agreements that are inherently flawed and relegated to mediocre achievement. Such self-dishonesty can even lead to the creation of agreements that will inevitably provoke angry disagreement, the antithesis of their intended formation.

It is also essential that we get a feeling for the other party's intent. Notwithstanding the content of what is verbally expressed, signals which indicate intent may be broadcast unconsciously and can become apparent to us in unusual contexts. For example, any remark made or action taken by the other party which feels "off" to us cannot be ignored or overlooked even though our mind is determined to reach an agreement based upon the literal meaning of the words which are being used to describe the party's intent. When anything arises which appears to be inconsistent with the other party's verbalized intentions, we can allow our feeling nature to reflect on the inconsistency and let our intuition decide whether or not to continue to pursue an agreement with this person.

After we have identified the feelings underlying our inner motivations and our concerns about the motivations of the other party, we can then cross another equally challenging bridge by expressing these feelings to the other party. If we express these feelings with anything less than unmitigated, if not graphic, honesty, we risk an agreement that will give us muddled results to match our muddled intent.

If we have preliminarily decided to go ahead with the agreement, we may want to talk about any hesitation that we initially had in order to expose and come to terms with any ulterior motives or hidden agendas the other party might have. Until these feelings of concern are addressed, a lasting agreement may be difficult to achieve. In fact, any agreement reached without this clearing will likely contain the seeds of its untimely, and perhaps contentious, demise.

When we were younger, many of us learned that the honest expression of our feelings was either unacceptable or forbidden. Verbalization of exactly how we felt was usually not approved by most of our authority figures and could easily result in psychological or even corporal punishment. Later in life, some of us continued to avoid the honest expression of our feelings because we believed that if we tell it like it is, either love would be withheld from us or our truth would cause other people to be angry or feel hurt. We therefore would keep quiet and slowly became separated from our feelings which told us the truth. As our desire to be honest waned, our relationships became more and more superficial. Many of us became "nice" people who could not go any deeper with another person than conversations about the weather, sports or the latest gossip. The agreements we would make with others likewise suffered from a lack of the benefit of our full commitment to truth and intimacy.

To now break this life-pattern requires courage and determination which may seem well out of reach, yet to the extent we can do it, the likelihood of achieving successful legal agreements will be accordingly increased.

Lawyers can help facilitate honesty by encouraging their clients to get in touch with and describe their feelings about their real motivations, about the other party, about the stated purpose of the agreement and about the critical terms of the agreement.

Lawyers can also give their clients honest feedback concerning how the lawyer feels about the proposed agreement and how it does or does not appear to square with the client's stated intent. This reciprocal process will usually require lawyers to get in touch with their own feelings at a gut level and to get, at least temporarily, out of their heads. It is relatively easy to find a rational and logical basis for an agreement. It is much more challenging to identify what feelings an agreement, or a particular part of it, evoke. It may also be a little scary for lawyers to venture into the realm of honest expression of feelings for fear their clients may take their business elsewhere.

On the other hand, many clients will appreciate any offered insight which can positively transform and strengthen their agreements. Lawyers may have to accept that they cannot reap the benefits of uncompromising honesty without risking the loss of clients who do not want to face the truth. Lawyers who stay silent when the situation calls for their honest input are nothing more than amoral agents who help their clients implement their foggy intent by forming agreements inevitably doomed to failure. Win-win agreements usually match clients and lawyers boldly unafraid to speak their piece.

Technical Compliance

> Laws are like cobwebs, which may catch small
> flies, but let wasps and hornets break through.
> —Jonathan Swift, Anglo-Irish poet and
> satirist, from "A Critical Essay upon the
> Faculties of the Mind"

"Technical compliance" refers to those situations in which legal counsel is retained to help individuals or businesses comply with the technical requirements of the law, including corporation, securities, employment and tax laws, applications for tax-exempt or licensed status and compliance with safety, health or environmental standards.

Whether the myriad technical requirements of the law are unnecessarily burdensome or effectively serve society is not the subject of this discussion. Although the laws of the land are not always well written and sometimes favor special interest groups, they usually reflect our collective intent to right and prevent wrongs and to otherwise preserve the fundamental principles upon which our country was founded.

Many of our laws also reflect the personal intent of those who draft them, and usually the drafters hope to reflect the intent of the people who elect them. Of course, the final result does not always represent the collective intent of all of the people back home. Nevertheless, if we step back from any particular law, we could probably describe in a few words what the law generally intends to accomplish, even if the actual words are unartful, ambiguous or leave gaps in application which are commonly referred to as "loopholes". This general intent we will refer to as the "spirit" of the law.

When many of my clients ask me to help them technically comply with the law, they often assume that technical compliance means "minimum" compliance, in other words, to do only that amount of compliance which will minimally meet the requirements of the "letter" of the written words, no more and no less. The usual course of the minimum-compliance approach involves a rigorous search for loopholes which can sometimes exempt compliance altogether or at least water down compliance so that the spirit of the law is not echoed by those whose conduct it intends to regulate for the good of all.

Many lawyers and clients do not consider the spirit of the law when deciding how to comply with its requirements. This failure to reflect upon the spirit of the law and to evaluate compliance in terms of the client's general civic responsibility can often result in minimum compliance which is resented by those who, as a matter of principle, do not take advantage of loopholes and otherwise fully comply with the law. Aggressive minimum-compliance advice from lawyers competing for clientele can also undermine the general public's faith in lawyers and the ethical standards of the legal profession.

Many people comply with the spirit of the law because they cannot afford to hire a lawyer to avoid or minimize compliance. These people are naturally upset with those who have the resources to fully comply with the law yet spend money on lawyers to find loopholes. Some who can afford to hire a lawyer are also angered because they and their lawyer choose to comply with the spirit of the law while others greedily shirk their higher public responsibility. In any event, resentment continues to build toward lawyers and clients who conspire to find the shade behind the letter of the law.

On the other hand, not all laws deserve "spiritual" compliance and may deserve only to be accorded minimum compliance. Unfortunately, some laws are designed to oppress minorities, unfairly advance the causes of special interest groups or are just not well thought out. Finding loopholes exempting compliance with such laws may be the right thing to do. Also, people may reasonably disagree about whether the spirit of a particular law will enhance or degrade our quality of life or whether it truly serves our best collective interests.

Whether or not all people agree that the spirit of any particular law is universally beneficial is not necessarily important. What is more important is whether the person or group faced with complying with the particular law feels that the spirit of the law is worthwhile. If so, their compliance should follow their "spiritual" perspective even though it may go beyond minimal or token compliance. If not, minimum compliance may be the best approach.

Why is this important? Beyond the obvious public relations benefit to clients and their lawyers who comply fully with the law and scrupulously avoid loopholes, there is a deeper, more practical reason. Full compliance with a principle that resonates with the passion of the heart can infuse all who are employed by or deal with the complier with a sense of pride and trust that can ultimately translate into financial or emotional well-being. People trust people who follow their hearts especially if to do so means sacrifice. I have had many clients choose full compliance over an ostensibly beneficial loophole who thereafter receive a benefit from a totally unexpected source that more than offset the loss of the financial enticement offered by the loophole.

Most of us know this to be true in our daily lives. We admire those rare ones among us who doggedly follow their sense of right and wrong, even if we do not agree with them. We can trust that what they say is honest, that there is no hidden agenda, no bait and switch. We can trust that they will not cut corners because they believe in quality and service. If they say a product is worth buying, we are more likely to buy from them than buy from those who espouse one principle yet live another.

Living only by the letter of the law when it does not feel right to do so is also often short-sighted. Inevitably, this lack of inner harmony will be reflected in other aspects of our lives, and the short-term benefits gained from minimum compliance may keep other, more durable and rewarding benefits at bay. There is no known mathematical formula for this phenomenon, but we can probably recall many situations in our own lives which confirm that when our actions are inconsistent with our intent, they ultimately yield undesirable consequences.

How do we as lawyers and clients determine what the "spirit" of a law is? Clients can reflect on how they feel about the law in question. One of their inner voices may say, "I feel that this law is designed to promote the well-being of our society, and I agree with it in principle." Another voice may say, "Compliance with this law will inconvenience me or may actually pose financial or other hardship, and even though I agree with it in principle, I would like to avoid or minimize compliance."

The final decision will usually rest on the answer to the simple question: "Will compliance with only the letter of the law feel good to me?" If not, the only viable alternative is full compliance with the spirit of the law and acknowledgment that the letter of the law is only a minimum standard, a starting point, a baseline.

Lawyers can facilitate this process of clarifying the intent against which their clients' compliance will be measured by encouraging their clients to consider the broader context in which the particular law was enacted, to determine what its overall spirit is and to access how the client feels about minimum versus full compliance. The more we can relate to and discuss this larger perspective, the more we can consciously clarify the intent of our legal relationships with respect to the scope of our technical compliance.

Choosing a Lawyer

It is not, what a lawyer tells me, I may do; but
what humanity, reason, and justice, tells me I
ought to do.
  —Edmund Burke, Irish-born Whig politician
    and man of letters, from *On Conciliation
    with America*

No brilliance is needed in the law. Nothing but
common sense, and relatively clean finger nails.
  —John Mortimer, English novelist, barrister
    and playwright, from "A Voyage Round My
    Father"

Selecting the right lawyer can be, at best, a haphazard process. Despite popular opinion, all lawyers are *not* the same. The effectiveness of the lawyer-client relationship is directly proportional to the extent to which the lawyer and client can effectively relate with each other. A mismatch in a legal relationship can easily result in financial or emotional disaster. Clients can maximize their satisfaction with their choice of a lawyer by carefully considering the following suggestions.

Clients can talk to people who have had a direct experience with the lawyer they are considering and question them carefully about their opinion of the lawyer's integrity and honesty, sensitivity to feelings, ability to communicate clearly and responsively, commitment to fair dealing, general relationship skills, billing practices, and legacy of client satisfaction.

If an opinion based upon direct experience with the lawyer is unavailable, clients can notice how the lawyer's name comes to them and whether the circumstances surrounding the referral evoke a positive, negative or neutral feeling. If the feeling is positive or the information about the lawyer comes to the client serendipitously, the client can proceed to the interview stage. If neither, the client should probably remain open for another reference. I have had clients tell me that they decided to call me simply because they connected positively with my name listed in the "Attorneys" section of the Yellow Pages.

Upon meeting the lawyer, it is important for the client to remember that the decision whether or not to hire the lawyer is the client's, and, if hired, the lawyer will serve as the client's employee subject to termination at the client's pleasure. The client does not need to please the lawyer, and the client has every right to pointedly question the lawyer about his or her honesty and sensitivity to feelings. The client is entitled to ask direct questions and to demand clear and direct answers. The client does not have to be intimidated by the lawyer's legal education or social status. The client can seek to attain a complete understanding of and feeling about the lawyer's relevant knowledge and experience, overall integrity and relationship skills. To help minimize distracting nervousness during the initial meeting with the lawyer, the client can prepare in advance a list of specific questions designed to illuminate the person behind the law degree.

Clients can also avoid being misled by appearances. A lawyer's stylish clothes and plush office do not necessarily mean that the lawyer is equipped to handle the client's legal situation. On the other hand, some of the most honest and capable lawyers I know also happen to work for law firms that present an image of material success. Clients can ensure that they make the right choice by cutting through the lawyer's image to the essence of the human being. Clients must take as much time as is necessary for them to acquire an accurate feeling for that essence.

How the lawyer feels about the client's particular undertaking should be thoroughly questioned by the client, and the client must not be distracted by the lawyer's intellectual or legalistic responses. The client needs to know from the beginning how the lawyer honestly feels about the client's expressed goals, from both the lawyer's legal and intuitive perspectives.

The client must listen carefully to everything the lawyer says. If any of the words used by the lawyer do not ring true or otherwise make the client feel uneasy or uncertain about being in relationship with the lawyer, the client should immediately question the lawyer's use of the words. The lawyer's explanation may or may not cause the client's discordant feelings to dissipate. If not, the client may want to consider another lawyer.

The client also may not want to accept any legal conclusion drawn by the lawyer that defies the client's common sense without getting a clear understanding of the reason for the discrepancy. The client can request definition of legal terms and explanation of legal concepts so that the applicable law is reduced to a simple outline of step-by-step rules. It is totally permissible for clients to flaunt their ignorance.

The lawyer's competency to advise the client can also be investigated, taking into account the degree of difficulty of the legal task and the experience of the lawyer in handling similar matters. The client can ask the lawyer to explain in detail why the lawyer feels qualified to give legal counsel concerning the particular matter at hand.

The client can stay in touch with his or her body throughout the initial interview of the lawyer, for it may register feelings about the lawyer and about what the lawyer says. For example, does the client feel disgusted when the lawyer makes a cruel or deprecating remark about another person? Does the client's skin crawl when the lawyer attempts to be charming or flirtatious?

The client can also monitor thoughts that spontaneously occur to the client which question or support the prospective relationship. For example, does the thought "This doesn't feel right" occur to the client when the lawyer is pushing the most aggressive legal alternative available while assuring the client that its success is certain.

These thoughts and physical sensations may be extremely subtle or fleeting, but none of them are irrelevant. In fact, they may contain information more important to the client's choice of a lawyer than the logical processes of the client's rational mind which may tend to dismiss such intuitive flashes as mere anomalies. When there are inconsistencies between the conclusions drawn by the client's rational mind and these other, more spontaneous indicators of whether the particular lawyer is the best choice for the client, the client usually will be best served by spontaneity, especially when the feelings are negative.

I have had many clients come to me because their relationships with their lawyers were floundering. In almost every case, each of them recalled something about their lawyer that bothered them from the beginning, and many admitted that they knew early on that something was amiss but failed to act on their feelings and withdraw from the relationship.

Also, just because I feel that I would be the best lawyer for a client does not necessarily make it so. I am now thankful when a client chooses not to hire me because I know that to continue an incompatible relationship can often prove to be both unsatisfying and costly. Neither person can have any misgivings, however slight, about being in relationship with the other if the relationship is to have a good chance for success.

Choosing a Client

I have noted that persons with bad judgment are
most insistent that we do what they think best.
—Lionel Abel, American playwright and
drama critic, from *Important Nonsense*

In law school, I was taught that the successful representation of my clients would depend upon my ability to apply legal precedent to the "facts" of a situation rather than on my ability to recognize and honor in every "fact" situation the legal principles which serve the highest and the best in all of us. I was given endless instruction about how to analyze and solve clients' legal problems and virtually no help with evaluating whether or not I should agree to participate in their solution in the first place.

Ideally, laws are enacted to help us relate compassionately and fairly among ourselves, to ensure that we achieve the best out of our relationships with each other, individually and collectively. I naively believed that all I had to do was light the moral path, and my clients would obligingly follow. However, when I graduated from law school, I had little understanding of how to choose clients who shared my perception of how the law was designed to serve the highest good.

In my early years of practice, I would occasionally represent people of questionable integrity who had questionable undertakings and rationalize that they were entitled to have legal representation, and if it wasn't me, it would be someone else, so why not me? As a result, I would inevitably allow myself to be manipulated into representing these clients in situations where I was being used to take undue advantage of someone who could not afford to fight back. By the time I finally managed to extricate myself, I always felt somewhat tarnished by my failure to say "No!" in the beginning.

I have since learned that although every person may be entitled to legal representation, the people who offend my sense of
right and wrong do not have to be represented by me. I do not
have to practice law as a hired gun or puppet. My license to practice law does not require me to suspend my right to follow my
conscience. If enough lawyers say "no", maybe the current level
of client amorality will begin to decline, and some of the lost faith
in lawyers can be restored.

A lawyer choosing whether or not to serve a client can scru-
tinize the prospective client through the lawyer's feeling, as well
as mental, sensors. This intuitive evaluation of the client includes
consideration of the emotional state and intent of the client. If
the legal service contemplates technical compliance, the lawyer
can reflect upon how the client's intent squares with the spirit
of the law; if dispute resolution, how the client's intent demon-
strates an earnest desire to reasonably resolve the dispute; and
if agreement formation, how the client's intent reflects a commitment to unbridled honesty.

The lawyer can compassionately tune in to the emotional state
of the client without prematurely responding to the client's plea
for rescue. It is important for the lawyer to remain detached from
the emotions which are motivating the client to seek legal advice.
The habit patterns which are triggering the client's emotions may
be coloring the client's ability to realistically evaluate the present situation, and the lawyer can usually better serve the client
from a perspective outside of the client's emotional energy field.
The lawyer can, however, help the client identify the feelings
behind the client's emotional state to enable the client to more
clearly articulate the client's true intent and how this intent can
best be realized, with or without legal means.

The lawyer can also get in touch with his or her own feelings
about the advisability of supporting and promoting the client's
intent in the context of a professional relationship. The lawyer

can weigh the client's bottom-line intent with the lawyer's inner sense of truth and justice.

The lawyer can also determine if the client's intent comports with the lawyer's perception of the spirit of the laws involved, for if it does not, any ensuing relationship may compromise the heartfelt values of both. Any such disparity is also likely to impede the relationship's success. Even if the client's intent is not necessarily dishonest, it may appear to others to lack integrity if the values of the lawyer and the client are not harmonious.

If the lawyer's sense of the spirit of the law or what is fair and just in the situation at hand differs from that of the client, the lawyer may want to express the difference to the client in order to reconcile any misunderstanding. If there are still fundamental differences concerning intrinsic values, the lawyer may want to decline the employment and make it clear to the client why. Refusal of representation, whenever appropriate, is probably the single most challenging thing a lawyer can ever do and is one of the most important issues raised in this book.

In law school, many law students never learn how to facilitate active exploration of their feelings or those of their clients in order to achieve a commonality of intent in their professional relationships. Many people are drawn to the legal profession because they have lost touch with the wisdom of their own feelings and are more comfortable relating to others through dispassionate intellect. Most law schools are not presently equipped to heal this disconnection. Until lawyers learn how to access their own feelings so that they can determine whether or not they can honestly and ethically participate in a client's cause, it will be difficult to say "no". Until lawyers learn how to distinguish between the way the mind works and the way the heart works and how the two work together, the jokes about lawyers will continue to reflect our culture's disappointment with a profession ostensibly dedicated to ethical and ennobling service.

Even though lawyers may still choose to remain ignorant of

their feeling nature, there is one side effect of the consistent denial of feelings in legal relationships that can no longer be overlooked. Historically, many relationships with lawyers have felt as abstract as the legal advice given, disconnected from the emotions and feelings stirring in the client. Consequently, clients have seldom trusted lawyers with their feelings. Many clients also cannot confidently entrust their feelings to lawyers who do not follow their own feelings, their own sense of right and wrong, and who do not have the integrity to say "no" to legal undertakings which are inconsistent with their innermost values.

To routinely make decisions that take into account feelings usually requires commitment and courage, commitment to examine and change lifetime habits of relating and courage to trust that saying "no" can ultimately be more rewarding than the prospect of immediate financial gain. To this day, when I say "no" to someone who wants to hire me, I still have to deal with my inner voice of fear that tells me I cannot afford to turn away a paying client.

Even though cultivation of commitment and courage is an individual process for each lawyer, law schools can directly address these issues by incorporating into the academic curriculum the study of the psychological dynamics of human relationship and by encouraging students to look inwardly and follow the highest of ethical and moral standards when deciding to represent a client.

If public confidence in the legal system is to be restored, lawyers must decline to represent people and causes that offend the lawyer's conscience. Declining representation should also extend to any particular aspect of the representation that goes against the lawyer's fundamental sense of what is right. Only through a clear and unequivocal message to the client kingdom can the legal profession rebuild and maintain a high standard of ethical and moral integrity and regain the public's trust.

Boundaries and Ground Rules

> Life is a process of moving from environmental support to self-support. From puberty on, growing up and becoming mature means standing on one's two feet and being independent and self-supporting. No relationship is healthy if it is based on incompleteness and neediness. Healthy relationships are mature, which means equal and self-responsible.
>
> ...Furthermore, in a healthy and committed relationship each partner has a commitment to discipline. Each is self-disciplined and is willing to apply discipline to the relationship.
>
> —John Bradshaw, from *Bradshaw On: The Family*

Lawyers and clients can help each other delineate the professional and interpersonal boundaries of their legal relationships and establish the ground rules which will ensure that these boundaries are respected. From the professional perspective, the lawyer needs to know exactly what the client wants the lawyer to do. Nothing can be left to assumption. The client needs to know exactly what steps the lawyer will take on the client's behalf and why. The description of each of the steps that are to be taken must be reduced to its simplest terms, no distracting "legalese".

One of the tasks of a lawyer is to educate the client concerning all of the available legal and non-legal alternatives and then allow the client to take responsibility for and make the final decision. Because lawyers can easily, even though unintentionally, manipulate their clients' decisions, by withholding bits of legal knowledge or by unduly emphasizing the selection of one alternative over another, the client can make it clear to the lawyer at the beginning of the relationship that the client wants the lawyer to lay all of the cards on the table throughout the representation. The lawyer can then diligently supply complete information and provide the client with a thorough legal education. Only then can the client make full and informed decisions.

The client also needs to know the full range of the legal and practical consequences that could result from each step the lawyer may take on the client's behalf, so the client can decide whether or not the lawyer should be authorized to undertake any particular action (or inaction) affecting the client's interests. If the client wants to give the lawyer authority to exercise the lawyer's discretion under certain circumstances, the scope of the discretion should be carefully outlined, in writing when feasible.

Lawyers are not wiser than their clients. Most clients inherently know this but are still afraid to contradict their lawyer when their lawyer says or does something that does not feel right to the client. Even though they may willingly abdicate their personal power, clients are naturally resentful when they allow a lawyer to assume power over them. Lawyers sometimes try to overplay the importance of their legal knowledge out of fear that their clients might realize that they are just as smart as the lawyers, so why use them? In order to avoid this confusion, it is important for the lawyer and the client to dispel the myth that legal knowledge is superior to common sense and to commit to a mutual undertaking as peers who bring different but equally valuable perspectives to the relationship.

As a part of this commitment, the lawyer and client can also agree to relate to each other on the common ground of feelings. Each can agree to disclose their feelings as they apply to the purpose of the professional relationship, and each can agree to elicit and consider the feelings of the other throughout the relationship even if those feelings may defy legal logic or even seem bizarre or irrational.

The establishment of these boundaries and ground rules can

create a healthier atmosphere within which decision-making can be aligned with the feelings of both parties. At the very least, each can know that the relationship will encourage the expression of feelings as an integral aspect of the legal process.

Part of the reason for the current frustration with lawyers is that lawyers are often viewed as amoral technicians who mechanically manipulate laws that seem overwhelming in number and unfair in application. Because of the prevalence of this perspective, it is natural that few believe that lawyers can be sensitive to the feelings of those whose lives are directly affected by the legal system. Such sensitivity is, in fact, sorely lacking, and if the legal system is ever going to reconnect with the people to whom it is dedicated to serve, channels for listening to and accounting for these feelings have to be opened in virtually every lawyer-client relationship.

Cosmetic tinkering with improvements in client communication, client education and better billing practices can never alone accomplish this reconnection. Only people, lawyers and clients, focusing inward, relationship by relationship, can restore to the legal system a sensitivity to the value of intuitive feelings, what feels "right". Emphasizing the value of feelings in our professional relationships can result in legal decisions which enhance the quality of our lives. The cumulative effect of such legal decisions can ultimately transform the way we relate to each other in almost any legal context. Even though positive changes may manifest slowly over time, and each increment of movement toward feeling-based legal decisions may be very small and sometimes very subtle, the legal system can cleanse itself from the inside out if we are honest and vocal about what is truly important to us and if following our conscience is its own reward.

From an interpersonal perspective, the lawyer and the client can strive to create a relationship that will provide opportunities to make legal decisions that reflect life-enhancing values. The lawyer and the client can achieve this goal if their interpersonal relationship is free from distracting mental and behavioral habits, such as sexual innuendos, patriarchal overtones, victim-rescuer patterns and shadow projections.

Sexual innuendos made by men are, by definition, comments with patriarchal overtones. Patriarchal overtones also include remarks made by men which indicate disrespect for or condescension toward women. The offensiveness of these remarks can be clearly communicated to the offender. "Anti-male" remarks made by women also have no place in a legal relationship.

Victim-rescuer patterns and shadow projections are more challenging to deal with because they are usually well buried in the unconscious. Nevertheless, when they arise, they can be identified for what they are, habitual tendencies that are adversely affecting the success of the relationship. Accurately labeling a habit is the first step toward changing it. Habits are, by definition, unconscious and will repeat themselves unless they are explicitly made conscious. Embarrassment, anger and denial may follow the exposure of habitual behavior, but the behavior will usually change nevertheless.

When a victim inappropriately seeks rescue from a lawyer, the lawyer can clearly indicate to the client that the lawyer is not in the rescue business and that the client is expected to take full responsibility for all of the decisions made in the relationship.

When a client has a lawyer who wants to be the client's savior and who inflates the likelihood of success of the client's legal cause, the client can make it clear that the client only wants the lawyer to give advice which is practical and realistic. If the lawyer wants to do more for the client than feels necessary under the circumstances, the client can closely question the reason for the lawyer's expansive plans and prescribe clear limits of authority.

The client's shadow may also be projected onto the lawyer or the lawyer's shadow onto the client, or both projections can take place simultaneously. When this happens, there is likely to be a temptation to blame the other person for any difficulties the legal relationship may be experiencing. The person projecting blame can be encouraged by the one being blamed to realize that the energy it takes to blame and be angry might be better directed toward resolving the legal challenge facing the relationship.

The person who is the object of the other's blame can also refuse to accept or identify with it. For example, if a client were to blame a lawyer for the client's seemingly untenable legal situation, the lawyer need not respond to the blame with defensive anger. The lawyer can sympathize with the client's frustration yet refuse to identify with the client's criticism or to otherwise take it personally. Instead of lashing back at the client, the lawyer can agree that the client is understandably upset but is taking it out on the wrong person and let the client know that it does not feel good. The lawyer can then suggest that they focus on the real source of the client's apprehension and work together to make things different.

Conversely, a lawyer could blame a client for failing to tell the lawyer about a critical fact which, if known, might have caused the lawyer to recommend another course of action. If the lawyer cannot claim responsibility for failing to elicit the critical fact from the client, the lawyer may project his or her fear of not being perfect onto the client and hold the client responsible for the lawyer's mistake. The client's most effective response to such a projection may be to not take the accusation personally but nevertheless clearly communicate to the lawyer that the blame is misplaced and does not feel good. The client can then redirect the lawyer's attention to the task of solving the client's legal challenge.

In any event, shadow projections cannot be tolerated for very long without severely damaging the relationship. If they persist despite efforts to establish clear boundaries, the relationship may have to be terminated.

Sometimes this shadow material reveals itself at the beginning of the relationship. When a client makes disparaging remarks about another lawyer or about lawyers in general, the lawyer might want to make it clear that he or she is not to be associated with the client's general image of lawyers or with a prior unpleasant experience the client may have had. This may help the client to be thoughtful about any impulse that arises later in the relationship to automatically blame the lawyer when a setback occurs.

A lawyer may begin a relationship by using legal terms without defining them or by otherwise talking over the client's head. If this happens, the client can convey to the lawyer that he or she is not legally savvy and wants the lawyer to assume that everything must be explained in its most simple terms. This guideline will usually help the relationship avoid the costly mistakes that are caused by a lack of clear communication.

One of the most important boundary issues for both lawyers and clients is the bottom line, money. Many of us had parents who seldom talked about money in our presence. Perhaps that is why we may be reluctant to get graphic about money in our legal relationships. Money is a delicate subject in many lawyer-client encounters, and sometimes the demise of a legal relationship can be traced directly to a misunderstanding over money.

The most important money issues that need to be addressed when a legal relationship begins are "How much?" and "What for?" Both the lawyer and the client are responsible for making sure that there are clear and complete answers to these questions.

"How much?" means not only how much the lawyer charges but also how much the work will cost and how the client will pay for it. A lawyer's charges can be calculated in a number of ways, by the hour or by the job. If the lawyer is charging by the job, the fee can be a figure set in advance or it can be a percentage of an amount collected for a client. If a lawyer is charging by the hour, the lawyer is obligated to keep track of the actual time spent working on the client's matter and, when the work is completed, to bill the client an amount equal to the lawyer's hourly fee multiplied by the hours of actual work. The lawyer may also charge the client for out-of-pocket office expenses, associate lawyer, paralegal or secretarial time and state or local taxes. In any event, there is much explaining to be done by the lawyer and many questions to be asked by the client before the financial aspect of the relationship can be clearly agreed upon.

"What for?" is the other challenging question connected with money. The client usually wants to know exactly what the lawyer intends to do for the client that will earn the agreed-upon fee. Many clients leave their legal relationships with a bitter taste simply because they do not know where their money went. At the beginning of the relationship, it is imperative that the client know as precisely as possible what specific tasks the lawyer will be performing for which specific amounts of money. An open-ended agreement to charge fees by the hour is usually a set-up for disaster. The more clients can know in advance exactly what their bottom line will be, the more likely the legal relationship will be mutually satisfying.

4

Relationship through the Heart

Your vision will become clear only when you can look into your own heart. . . .Who looks outside, dreams; who looks inside, awakes.
—Carl Jung, to a patient, quoted in *Letters Vol. I*, ed. by Gerhard Adler

The Essence of Legal Relationship

> My request, my appeal, is that you try as much
> as you can to develop compassion, love, and
> respect for others, to share others' suffering, to
> have more concern for others' welfare, and to
> become less selfish. Whether you believe in
> God or not, in Buddha or not, does not matter.
> The important thing is to have a good heart, a
> warm heart, in daily life. This is the principle
> of life.
>> —The Fourteenth Dalai Lama, from *Kindness,
>> Clarity and Insight*

> The clear bead at the center changes everything.
> There are no edges to my loving now.
> I've heard it said there's a window that opens
> from one mind to another,
> but if there's no wall, there's no need
> for fitting the window, or the latch.
>> —Jelaluddin Rumi, Persian poet and mystic,
>> from *Open Secret*

If one only read the daily newspaper, it would appear that most
people perceive interpersonal relationship as an interaction
between two separate and independent individuals and that it is
from this limited perspective that most people apply their
acquired relationship skills, to a you and a me, to an us and a
them.

My personal and professional experience tells me that most
legal relationships in our culture also perpetuate the myth of
separateness. Lawyers are generally conditioned to approach their
professional relationships with the assumption that there must be
a you *versus* a me. They are trained at law school to analyze
human interactions by delineating the actors according to legal

roles that are usually oppositional. Many clients are conditioned by our culture to placidly accept the roles that lawyers assign to them.

For most of my professional career, I have struggled to find a comfortable place within a legal system that I perceived to be adversarial in nature. Fresh out of law school, I entered the legal fray primed for competition. I defended indigent juveniles and later indigent adults charged with felony crimes. I battled fervently for my underprivileged clients against judges and prosecutors to ensure that the constitutional rights of every citizen remained inviolate. When I later entered private practice and began representing people in a wide variety of personal and business contexts, I continued to relate to my clients as if I were their knight-errant, always pitted against other people or other forces. However, over time, the lines that seemed to separate me from my clients and us from others began to blur, and I found it more and more difficult to justify legal solutions that were fashioned to perpetuate this sense of competitive separateness.

After about ten years of mixed success with less competitive approaches, I went through an intense period of personal crises that began to crack my own defenses of personal isolation. It slowly began to dawn on me that perhaps I was intertwined with others at a much deeper level than I had thought possible and that what I did to others, I was also doing to myself.

This revelation also spilled over into my professional life. I began to look at clients as if they might also be extensions of me, and I began to consider the possibility that their legal challenges were all part of a larger whole that could be more easily balanced when we consciously enlarged our perspectives. The more I allow myself to entertain this possibility, the more synergistic the legal solutions become and the more satisfied are my clients. Paradoxically, I have also discovered that I can still set firm interpersonal boundaries and establish definite guidelines with my clients while we simultaneously imagine legal solutions that account for the inseparability of the human spirit.

This experience has convinced me that real and fundamental change in the legal system can occur when we understand that the isolation and separateness that we feel coming into a legal relationship can begin to dissipate when we view everything that is happening in our world as an extension of us instead of something outside of us doing something to us.

When we get beyond the illusion of "us versus them", we can begin to see "us in them" and treat us in them with more understanding and compassion. This shift in perspective can help lawyers and clients solve legal problems at a much deeper level and can also help them deal more compassionately with others in the course of their joint undertaking.

The Role of the Heart

Opinion is ultimately determined by the feelings,
and not by the intellect.
  —Herbert Spencer, English philosopher, from
  Social Statics

So the heart be right, it is no matter
which way the head lies.
  —Sir Walter Raleigh, at his execution, on
  being asked which way he preferred to lay
  his head, quoted in *Sir Walter Raleigh*
  by W. Stebbing

To help our mind dissolve its tendency to view legal relationship only as separateness, we can allow our "other source" of intelligence to connect us with the reality of our unity. That "other source" is our intuition which some have described as "thinking through the heart". Our heart always knows when we are moving toward that state of non-duality which many call love. If allowed to speak, our heart can guide us to legal decisions that are more in alignment with the reality of our interrelatedness.

Our heart attunes us to our membership in the cosmos and enables our abstract mind to connect with our humanity here on Earth. If we consciously filter our mental concepts through the compassionate heart when we make legal decisions, we may discover that the best solution is usually the one which ensures the highest good for all people who may be affected by it.

The introduction of the compassionate heart into our legal relationships can be accomplished through our determination to trust that by serving others and eliminating their suffering we are also serving ourselves. Many of us know this feeling. It is not totally foreign to our personal experience. Most of us can recall at least one occasion in our lives when we have helped another person selflessly, without motive or conditions, and have felt the joy that resulted when we momentarily forgot that there was a giver and a receiver. When we experienced this feeling, we touched the thread of compassion which connects all human hearts.

An increase in the frequency of this experience may require considerable effort on our part to change how we look at other people, but what more truly satisfying goal is there?

Each thought, word or deed we entertain can consciously be passed through the heart. Our intuitive feelings can then arise spontaneously. Destructive emotions may also surface and attempt to divert our attention from our feelings, but when we calm these emotions, we can usually determine which of our intuitive solutions feels most likely to serve the highest good. Lawyers and clients can openly discuss with each other the goals of their decision-making process. For such a discussion to be productive, feelings and intellectual concepts must be held in equal esteem. Denial of feelings can result in legal decisions which will harm people and the earth. For example, when we deny that a scheme to avoid compliance with pollution controls will ultimately result in ecological deterioration, we may fail to investigate legal solutions that serve both the client and the environment. Denial of the intellect can result in decisions which are not practical and therefore cannot help people and the earth. At the other extreme, wholesale rejection of scientific thinking can hinder the development of technology that could foster environmental harmony.

The heart organ is not centered in the body by accident. It symbolizes the link between two worlds, our feeling nature, grounded in the earth, and our mental nature, reaching out to the etheric realm of ideas. The balance we want to achieve requires our mind to "think through the heart". This type of thinking can occur when the constant and habitual chatter of the mind slows long enough to permit entry of thoughts generated by our intuition. Many Eastern traditions have long used meditation techniques to consciously still the mind in order to access enlightened wisdom.

I was trained in law school to break a legal problem into manageable component parts and arrive at a solution by explaining and organizing the components in a logically coherent fashion. I was seldom asked to consider my own feelings about the law or my own sense of morality or justice. The emphasis in law school was more on the technically correct solution that was consistent with legal precedent and less on a solution that would accommodate human feelings or moral introspection.

When I first began to practice law and for many years thereafter, I tended to rigidly force my clients' square human problems into round legal holes. I often only paid attention to the ninety-nine facts that would enable me to categorize the problem in such a way that would yield a legally perfect solution. I seldom paid attention to the one fact which might be inconsistent with my technical masterpiece. Usually that conveniently overlooked fact was critically connected to my feelings or the feelings of my client. I was terrified that those feelings might be expressed because I would have to deal with them, and I did not know how. So the feelings would remain unexpressed, the legally perfect solution would be put into effect, and everyone would go their own way with a nagging feeling of incompletion.

Our minds usually cannot lead us through the mist alone. Without the balance of our intuitive feelings, our minds are likely to continue to abstractly create a climate for violence and destruction while viewing the carnage from a distance as if in a dream. The mind is often like a television set that brings us scenes of unspeakable horrors from around the world which we then calmly discuss over dinner. We are removed one step from the humanity of the experience.

One way for lawyers and clients to get beyond the metaphor of the television set is to describe what the impact of their legal decisions might feel like from the perspective of those who would be affected by them. Only when there is an empathetic understanding of how another might feel were the contemplated decision to be implemented can the decision makers have compassion for those who may experience the ultimate consequences of the decision.

Another way to get to the same place is to always measure legal decisions in terms of the highest good. This requires spiritual knowledge, that all life is interdependent and that every thought, word or deed must be motivated by compassion. This is a rigorous standard by any means, but it will raise the octave of any professional endeavor.

Reliance on the heart does not mean we should rescue victims, nor does it mean we cannot speak the truth even though someone's feelings may be hurt. Active compassion for the highest good does, however, require firm resolve and courage of conviction.

From the day of our birth, most of us have been conditioned by our culture to think our way through most of life's challenges. Many of us have found this approach lacking and stressful. We can now begin to heal ourselves and our relationships by talking to each other about our feelings and thinking through our heart. It may be awkward at first, but we can begin by saying "I feel" and mean it.

Emotions and Feelings

> The power to feel allows each of us to know
> our own unique spontaneous reality. Emotions
> are tools that allow us to be fully aware of
> where we are in fulfilling our needs.
> —John Bradshaw, from *Bradshaw On: The*
> *Family*

Many of my professional relationships begin with my new client telling me a very personal story that is full of emotion. In my early days of legal practice, I would often get sidetracked by the client's emotions and offer legal advice which was designed, at least in part, to make the client feel better emotionally. I regretted almost every time I did this because my advice was invariably inadequate or incomplete. I have since realized that my best legal advice discriminates between emotions and feelings.

Our emotions can help us meet our present needs. However, if we regularly repress or deny our emotions, they can cause our present experience to be contaminated by our unresolved past experiences, making it difficult to identify, much less meet, our present needs.

When our emotions arise habitually in response to events which remind us of a past experience, they can also become addictive in nature. That is, we can become addicted to either the bodily sensation or the behavior that we associate with the emotion. When our emotional habits are addictive, they can also block our intuitive feelings and thus impair our ability to perceive people and events clearly.

The physical stimulation caused by an emotion can distract the body's receptors from any opportunity to detect subtle feelings or flashes of intuition concerning our present experience. When

this occurs, we are deprived of the information necessary to cor-
rectly evaluate our present experience so that we can make decisions which fully meet our current needs. Our intuitive feelings
are still broadcasting; they are just harder for us to decipher
amidst our emotional static.

When a strong emotion is present in the lawyer-client relationship, the relationship is faced with the challenge of how to deal
with the emotion without impairing the parties' abilities to access
their feelings and thus jeopardizing the relationship's likelihood
of success.

One effective way to clear our intuitive channels is to express
our emotions at the time they occur. In a legal relationship, the
understanding between lawyer and client can deepen and even
reveal intuitive pearls when the expression of emotions is
encouraged without fear of judgment. Useful information can
surface when the other person listens compassionately and
acknowledges that the emotion is a real and important experience for the person expressing it. The listener can also allow the
expression of the emotion to lead to the identification of an underlying feeling that might be more relevant to the present legal
decision-making process. In the space following the expression
of an emotion, the feelings which are more specific to the present situation are often more easily accessible. For example, fear
may lead to a realization about how personal power has been surrendered or projected and what positive steps can be taken to
reclaim it. Anger may give way to an understanding of what may
have motivated the offender and what constructive alternatives can
be explored to repair the breach.

Many legal relationships are, like most other relationships, full
of emotional activity, repressed and expressed. Often clients
express their emotions and feelings to lawyers who deny theirs.
It is little wonder that many people walk away from legal relationships shaking their heads and asking themselves, "What was
that?" Even though they may not be able to pinpoint the reason

for their equivocal experience, they feel that most lawyers lack compassion and do not know how to relate to their emotions and feelings.

Fortunately, all lawyers do not cynically avoid emotions and feelings. Many simply do not know how to access them, much less work with the emotions and feelings of their clients, in the context of a professional relationship. Many of those lawyers who really are cynical unconsciously adopt their cynicism as a device to protect their own feelings and emotions from exposure to the critical judgment of others.

If the legal profession is to conscientiously serve the planet into the next century, lawyers can no longer deny that the service they are sworn to provide requires an intimate understanding of the psychology of human relationship and the interpersonal skills that can incorporate and account for emotions and feelings in every legal decision.

Until the legal profession formally requires lawyers to be educated in the psychology of human interrelationship, each lawyer can decide whether or not to individually face his or her own fears about working directly with emotions and feelings and to actively explore how to effectively help clients translate their emotions and feelings into healthy legal decisions.

Clients can also stop claiming that they are unwitting victims of a cruel and callous legal system. If they are disappointed with the lack of attention being paid by their lawyers to their emotions and feelings, they must simply demand more attention. They do not have to let their lawyers discount their emotions or their feelings. They do not have to succumb to legal decisions which do not feel right just because their lawyers profess superior intellectual knowledge.

While petitioning these deaf legal ears, clients must also choose to not remain mired in their emotions. They must consciously encourage their emotions to lead to intuitive feelings so that even the most cynical of lawyers can appreciate the transition.

Conflict and Anger

So rather than try to 'behave' and not feel our
rage or rather than using it to burn down every
living thing in a hundred-mile radius, it is
better to first ask rage to take a seat with us,
have some tea, talk a while so we can find out
what summoned this visitor.
—Clarissa Pinkola Estes, Ph.D., from *Women
Who Run With the Wolves*

Our legal system subtly promotes the emotion of anger, because
anger generally causes and prolongs conflict, and prolonged legal
conflict usually generates more legal fees. Many legal conflicts
cannot be economically resolved because the participants in the
conflict do not know how to deal with their anger. In our society, most of us have not learned how to view anger as a door
to the deeper level of understanding that we are responsible for
the world that we create for ourselves, over and over again.
Instead of learning how conflict, the expression of disagreement,
can lead to harmony, many of us have embraced the example set
by our role models and peers to withhold feelings, hang on to
anger and ride it to self-destruction.

I have met many prospective clients who were so overwhelmed
by anger that they were unable to consider any but the most
aggressive legal action. When I agreed to participate in their
desire for legal revenge, I would always regret my decision. Compromise was usually out of the question, and these clients were
seldom inclined to consider alternatives that would be beneficial
.if they felt that their antagonist would also derive benefit. Although
anger is usually a factor in most legal disputes, I most often encountered explosive, self-destructive anger in the context of a divorce
or the break-up of a long-standing business relationship.

My own anger has also created problems for some of my clients. Especially early in my career, I would often get angry at an authority figure, such as a governmental bureaucrat, a judge or another lawyer. Because I had not consciously dealt with my anger toward authority figures that I acquired in childhood, the intensity of my anger would usually be disproportionate to the situation at hand and would often interfere with my ability to effectively represent my client.

Conflict and anger are not necessarily synonymous. Conflict is disagreement. Anger can arise when we delay our disagreement and do not simultaneously express it with the feeling that tells us that we disagree. Anger can also be a spontaneous emotion, but here we will examine anger in the context of our failure to contemporaneously express a feeling of displeasure or disagreement with another.

Anger can also be an intense and sometimes violent emotional response to a perceived boundary violation such as hurtful or degrading behavior. Anger may also be used to aggressively manipulate or control those who have difficulty standing up to anger directed at them. Anger often distorts communication and can escalate a relatively benign conflict of opinions into a harmful and abusive encounter.

The word "anger" has several roots. One is from the Old English word "enge" which means "narrow". When we perceive that another person is violating our physical or psychological airspace, we may defend ourself with anger because our identity as an individual is being threatened. When we narrowly view the world as being separate and apart from us, we may see ourself as isolated, vulnerable and surrounded by potentially hostile forces. This, of course, is an illusion. We are not separate nor is there anything to protect, yet our defensive anger can further narrow our perception of reality and consequently exclude any other, more compassionate possibilities.

"Anger" is also derived from the Old Norse (Old Icelandic)

word "angr" which means "troubled" or "afflicted". This derivation suggests that our anger is directly connected with our
physical body. In other words, our body becomes "troubled" or
"afflicted" with this emotion because it senses a threat to its physical integrity.

"Anger", as well as the word "anxious", is also derived from
the Latin word "angere" which means "to strangle" or "to
choke". This derivation connects the emotion of anger with the
failure to get air through the throat and with the anxiety that
accompanies a sensation of choking. When we "choke" on our
words, anger arises. This illustrates why anger can result when
we fail to express our disagreement. The energy behind the disagreement is choked back into the body. It usually cannot dissipate until it is expressed. This energy does not idly lie in wait.
It can feed recurring angry thoughts which generate even more
energy, and we often become more and more anxious. When the
disagreement is eventually expressed, it is magnified by the force
of the accumulated energy behind it. In some people it may take
a tremendous build-up of energy before the words of disagreement finally explode through the throat. Usually, the longer the
suppression, the more violent the explosion. The explosion may
be directed toward people who had nothing to do with the initial
disagreement, yet who have the unfortunate honor of providing
"the last straw".

I am not suggesting that we should not passionately express
our disagreement nor protect ourselves against abuse. However,
when our passionate expression is not contemporaneous with our
feeling that registers disagreement and is held back to simmer
on the stove, the energy moving the passion can become disproportionate to our original disagreement.

Conflict, on the other hand, is often necessary for evolution-
ary progress to occur. Two different points of view will naturally
disagree before a synthesis or new viewpoint can result. Conflict
in legal relationships can result in creative problem solving so

long as the disagreements between the parties are clearly and fully stated. When the nature and scope of the disagreement is not explicitly expressed and the feelings behind the disagreement are repressed, anger may enter the conflict and pose a threat to the relationship.

Conflict need not be avoided in a legal relationship. Lawyers and clients can jointly endeavor to identify every point of disagreement between them regarding either the means or the ends of the relationship and to communicate to each other the feelings behind each of the divergent points of view.

Once expression of any disagreement occurs, the parties can strive to avoid angry responses which may impair the effectiveness of the relationship. Each can make a conscious effort to consider the positive potential of the other's contrary position and, if the contrary position is still not completely acceptable, to investigate the possibility of a new synthesis of what may initially appear to be incompatible. We can let go of any emotional attachment to the acceptance of our particular point of view and not react defensively. We can be passionate without letting ourself be threatened by another's rejection of our passion. Instead of angrily clinging to the old and the known, we can embrace disagreement as our path to the new and the unknown.

Many times the anger present in a lawyer-client relationship is directed at a person or persons outside of the relationship, usually because the lawyer and client believe that a boundary violation has occurred. Victims are often angry. Their anger is usually a device to mask their fear of taking responsibility for their actions. When directed at a persecutor, a victim's anger can distract the rescuer from noticing that the victim is afraid or unwilling to claim responsibility for the victim's plight.

Even though the boundary violation may seem real and the cause may appear to be just, a prospective rescuer can carefully consider the wisdom of joining in or even agreeing with a victim's anger. After honoring the victim's anger by allowing its expression, a compassionate listener can then guide the way to the deeper feelings that feed or need the anger. The optimum solution may reveal itself when the victim's hurt or fear that requires the protection of anger is directly addressed.

Because anger is also an affliction of the body, attention can be given to calming the body. In an office setting, a useful technique is to consciously allow the rhythm of the breath to ease the tension which coincides with the emotion. The breath is our body's connection with life and with each other. If we become aware of anger arising in ourself or in the other person, we can assist its processing by focusing on the rhythmic regulation of our breath. Our rhythmic breathing can have a calming effect on the anger that is present and can help create an environment that feels safer and less defensive.

If either the lawyer or the client persists in being angry, consideration can be given to terminating the relationship. Decisions made in a state of anger or agitation will ultimately be harmful to the decision-makers. Anger can be a useful emotion only if it brings our underlying feelings to the surface, but if it does not serve this purpose quickly, it can block our access to our intuition, causing us to miss a window of opportunity to reconcile the conflict.

Whether or not the anger being experienced *should* be contemporaneously expressed is discussed at length in Carol Tavris' excellent book, *Anger, The Misunderstood Emotion*. Tavris argues that it is not necessarily healthy to express chronic, aggressive or self-destructive anger. However, when anger arises in a legal relationship, I recommend its immediate expression before it builds in intensity because the effectiveness of the relationship will be impaired until it is cleared. Tavris provides some useful tips concerning how the anger can be effectively expressed: (1) direct the anger at its target (don't take it out on the wrong person); (2) its expression must restore our sense of justice; (3) it must change the behavior of the target or give us new insights;

(4) we and our target must speak the same anger language (usually express it from our point of view and avoid labeling the other person as "bad", for example, "I feel angry when you do/say that", instead of "I'm angry because you're a jerk"); and (5) its expression must not be of such intensity that would cause the target to retaliate angrily (its expression must not escalate the conflict).

Since anger, like most other emotions, is usually unconsciously associated with a past experience, it has a tendency to obscure our clear perception of present events. Our challenge in legal relationships is to see anger as an indicator of deeper feelings that must be addressed first if we are to fully understand what presently faces us. When anger is present, we have a choice. We can either let it serve to perpetuate our fear and isolation, or we can investigate why it is present and determine whether the belief system that supports it is still serving our best interests or requires adjustment.

Most of us can point to something in our lives to be angry about. However, if our legal system is ever going to fully serve us again, we have got to stop excessively indulging in an emotion that can only hurt us in the long run. It is natural to feel anger. Our bodies and minds hold complex memory patterns that unconsciously and illogically trigger anger. When our anger no longer consumes us nor determines our behavior in our legal relationships, we can begin to access the intuitive feelings that will lead us to higher ground.

Forgiveness

> He that cannot forgive others, breaks the bridge
> over which he must pass himself; for every man
> has need to be forgiven.
> —Lord Herbert, English philosopher and poet

> Life is an adventure in forgiveness.
> —Norman Cousins, American essayist and editor,
>   from "Saturday Review", April 15, 1978

In our culture, "forgiveness" and "law" are seldom mentioned in the same breath. Even those who press for legal reform rarely provide a place for forgiveness in their efforts to ameliorate the harshness of the legal process. Forgiveness is a little understood, if not suspicious, concept, and many people associate it with weakness or powerlessness. Many see forgiveness, like giving up anger, as an idea that would jeopardize the security of the personal boundaries that we have worked so hard to establish. Yet, if real and positive change in our legal relationships is to occur, we may have to finally understand what forgiveness really means and even begin to apply it liberally.

What is forgiveness? Is it throwing in the towel? Is it a fancy way of saying "I surrender"? Is it an abandonment of real and precious rights? Is it merely a way to justify our meek acquiescence to others in the face of their anger or other intimidating behavior?

Forgiveness means "to give up resentment against". In other words, in order to even consider forgiveness as an available legal option, we have to first admit that we are holding resentment against another. Resentment is a nice way of saying anger. Therefore, we can also say that if we are considering forgiveness as an option, we must first acknowledge that we are afflicted with anger, that what we have to give up resides within us.

The next question that follows from our acknowledgment that we are holding onto anger is "If we give up our anger, will we also give up our power?" This question can usually be answered if we examine who has control over our anger. If our anger is present in us when we are considering forgiveness, obviously we do not have control over our anger because we have allowed it to continue to remain present in us. If we believe that another person is responsible for the continued presence of our anger, then the other person must have the power to create anger within us, and we must therefore be helpless. So who really has the power over our anger? Do we want to reclaim power over our own anger, or do we want to give it away to others and be angry at their whim?

The answer is apparent from the question. The power to decide how we want to feel resides in our mastery of forgiveness. When we give up our resentment against another person, we are consciously choosing to not allow that person to exercise the power to make us angry. Forgiveness is really the acknowledgment that we are ultimately responsible for the world we create and how we feel about it. Once we fully accept that responsibility, we can then make conscious choices that can adjust our creation to align with our ideal of how we really want to live.

Similarly, when anger is present in a lawyer-client relationship and it is directed against another person or group of people outside of the relationship, those outside of the relationship have unwittingly been handed the power to block the lawyer's and the client's access to their collective intuitive resources which could otherwise inspire an innovative legal solution. For example, if my client and I are angered by the conduct of another lawyer and his or her client and we continue to relate to them through the emotion of anger, we may miss an opportunity to reconcile our differences. In any event, our perpetuation of an angry climate will delay the satisfactory achievement of our goals.

When we allow someone else to control our anger button and repeatedly push it, we will, of course, continue to direct our anger toward them. If we let others trigger our anger, we may also never understand why we are unable to end our relationship with them. Even if the relationship is terminated legally, it will be carried on afterward in the hearts and minds of the parties because the anger has not been released.

Lawyers and clients can help each other be more aware of how this works. Instead of seeking angry revenge and thereby perpetuating a relationship that no one really wants, lawyers and clients can terminate and sometimes even transform these destructive relationships by using the empowering tool of forgiveness.

Forgiveness does not usually come easy. First-time forgivers may soon discover that they have undertaken a warrior's task. Forgiveness does not automatically come by uttering words of forgiveness. We may find it difficult to let go of deeply ingrained and very comfortable habits. In fact, many of us may not know of any other way to relate, so we may also experience fear when we consider releasing our old friend resentment. Despite these challenges, the effort is worthwhile, as our attachment to resentment and anger toward another can be completely released if we learn how to forgive.

We should first be forgiving toward ourselves. Our anger has helped us be survivors, and we must honor it for that. Yet we must also begin to realize how, much of our creative energy we expend holding onto our anger long after the original offense has occurred. We usually churn through and replay our angry thoughts over and over again, while our unreleased anger may not even affect the person against whom it is directed. That person may be merrily going about their life while we gnash over old wounds and envision a hundred ways to express our anger and gain revenge. At what point in this process does our anger cease to serve us? At whatever that point is, our anger can begin to hurt, not help, us unless it is released.

Releasing anger does not mean rushing to the offender with outstretched arms. When we forgive another, we can choose what kind of relationship we want to have with that person, if any. If we choose not to be in relationship with the person whom we believe to have provoked our anger, we can end the relationship the moment we stop holding a negative image of the other person in our consciousness. We can literally neutralize our emotional connection to the other person. When we can completely release our resentment or anger toward the offender, we deprive the offender of any power to exercise control over us by triggering our anger at will.

One method of releasing a negative image is to substitute a positive one. Even though this may initially seem impossible, we may be willing to admit that our negative experience with the other person may have taught us something about ourself that can help us in similar situations in the future. If we can think of one positive lesson we have learned, then we may be able to acknowledge that, in a sense, our antagonist was our teacher. We can then be thankful for our lesson and release the negative tension that holds our antagonist in relationship with us.

If we choose to remain in the relationship, we must facilitate forgiveness by redirecting the energy we have invested in anger. One helpful technique is to put our anger in perspective. When we imagine how much worse the person could have harmed us, we can be thankful that the harm that was actually done was not as bad as it could have been. Another useful technique is to imagine ourselves in the shoes of the perpetrator. Again, we can put the aggrieving incident in perspective by compassionately considering the surrounding circumstances and emotional forces which could have caused the other person to act offensively. In either event, we can introduce the frailty of the human condition into our anger equation and begin to see the "bad guy" as a human being struggling to "get it right", yet making mistakes just like us.

When we begin to get a glimpse of what is behind the veil of our anger, our forgiveness is not just an intellectual exercise. Through forgiveness, we can actually encounter the frail essence of the person who is the object of our anger, and, by doing so, we may find a way to reconcile our differences and dissipate the fear that separated us in the first place. This is the fertile ground where miracles occur; where avowed enemies join hands as friends. Such a reconciliation may not happen for everyone. Many of us may just be content with the release of our anger and a healthy choice to go our separate ways. Yet, the possibilities cannot become unlimited until we completely let go of any need or desire we may have to remain angry.

Choices

The prologues are over. It is a question, now,
Of final belief. So, say that final belief
Must be in a fiction. It is time to choose.
  —Wallace Stevens, American poet, from
    "Asides on the Oboe"

I am rather like a mosquito in a nudist camp;
I know what I ought to do, but I don't know
where to begin.
  —Stephen Bayne, on becoming first executive
    officer of the Anglican Communion, quoted
    in "Time", January 25, 1960

Every step we take in a legal relationship draws us closer to a legal result that may or may not be what our heart truly desires. Despite what we may have been taught, we do have the power to choose the steps we take and the direction of our path. Mastery of this power requires an intimate understanding of each of the component parts of our individual input into the decision-making process and how they work together. The following is a discussion of some of the critical behavioral choices available to us as our legal relationships unfold.

The spiritual dimensions of this process are clearly delineated in Deepak Chopra's brilliant book, *The Seven Spiritual Laws of Success*. In order to facilitate the incorporation of these spiritual laws into our legal relationships, I suggest evaluating our critical behavioral choices in terms of our attitudes, thoughts, words and actions.

Attitude

Even if you're on the right track, you'll
get run over if you just sit there.
—Will Rogers

After a lawyer and a client initially clarify the relationship's
intent, they cannot afford to rest on their laurels. Simply defining intent does not necessarily insure its manifestation. I have had
many clients who had good intentions at the outset but could not
follow through because of their attitude.

For example, I have had a number of clients desiring to start
non-profit organizations who initially came to me expressing an
intent that was ostensibly committed to service to others. However, as their projects began to take form, their attitudes toward
the legal issues that arose along the way indicated that they were
becoming selfish and self-aggrandizing. In almost every case,
these clients never got their causes very far off the ground
because their attitudes in practice were not as selfless as their
ideals in theory.

Some of my clients have engaged my services to right a wrong
with an attitude of indignant outrage, and I later realized that I
was actually being manipulated by them to perpetrate an injustice.
I also know of lawyers who have exhibited unrealistically positive or "tough-guy" attitudes about the likelihood of their clients'
success in court even though win-win settlement offers were on
the table, and their clients never knew what hit them when they
lost.

I use "attitude" here to mean our state of being, our method
of relating, that expresses or translates our inner intent to the outer
world. In other words, our attitude will inevitably reveal whether
or not we really believe in our expressed intent. If our heart, our

intuition's message center, is not aligned with our verbalized intent, the inconsistency will usually show up in our attitude. Some of us have learned to mask or disguise our feelings by assuming superficial or fake attitudes. An attitude of superiority may be adopted to hide feelings of inferiority. An aggressive attitude may hide insecurity. We can become so accustomed to our false attitudes that we may find it difficult to remember the feelings that we are hiding. Some of us may deliberately use attitudes which are less than genuine to deceive or manipulate others. In any event, it can be very challenging for a client or a lawyer to determine if the other's attitude is consistent with the intent which has been voiced to map the path of the legal relationship.

If one of the parties is not committed to the manifestation of the relationship's intent, such lack of heart engagement will usually appear in the party's attitude, even despite elaborate attempts at disguise. Such lack of commitment may be revealed by an odd facial expression, a curious choice of words, a subtle intonation of speech or an inappropriate choice of action or inaction. Our intuition can usually detect such a slip.

In a legal relationship, no inconsistency, however slight, between intention and attitude can be discounted or ignored. If the purpose of the relationship is to have its best chance of being fulfilled, both the lawyer and the client may have to find the courage to directly question each other about the subtlest of inconsistencies in attitude. Periodic attitude checks can also encourage an ongoing review of the original intent of the parties and can enable the legal relationship to successfully adjust its original vision when necessary.

When we begin to trust the manifestation of our clear intent and consciously engage our attitude through our heart, we can also begin to raise the purpose of our intent to a higher level of humanitarian service. Many of us learned early on in our lives that it is virtually impossible to have what we want, that a clear vision of purpose would not necessarily help us materialize our desires, that life does not always respond to our intentions or attitudes. However, some of us have realized that it is not a coincidence that the quality of our lives directly reflects the quality of our attitude and behavior.

When we reconnect with our innate capacity to design our own destiny, we can consider what we want our destiny to really look like. We can then raise our vision to the highest and best we want out of life, for ourselves and for others. The short term can then give way to the long haul. We will naturally begin to aspire to achieve harmony and balance, with each other and with our environment. We will know that it is okay to be idealistic about life and to advocate our desire for peace in our immediate sphere of influence and beyond.

Open and ongoing discussion about our intentions and attitudes will also help elevate our legal relationships above cold analysis and mechanistic application of abstract legal principles. When we demand clear verbalization of intention and subsequent attitude checks in our legal relationships, we will help return our legal system to the realm of real live human beings who have real live feelings and who, deep down, desire a better world in which to live.

Thoughts

This phenomenal world...is nothing but
thought. When the world recedes from one's
view-that is when one is free from thought-
the mind enjoys the Bliss of the Self.
Conversely, when the world appears-that is
when thought occurs-the mind experiences
pain and anguish.
  —Ramana Maharshi, Indian saint, from
    Collected Works of Ramana Maharshi

A bad habit can be quickly changed....
A habit is the result of concentration of the
mind. You have been thinking in a certain way.
To form a new and good habit, just concentrate
in the opposite direction.
  —Paramahansa Yogananda, Indian saint, from
    Sayings of Paramahansa Yogananda

Most clients who come to me are dragging a bag of thoughts
which explain why they now find themselves in a law office, or
so they "think". Once the thoughts are taken out of the bag and
shown to me, we usually spend a great deal of time considering
new thoughts which may lead the way to a much more beneficial legal result than could ever have been achieved with the old
thoughts. When the clients are willing, we sometimes even
suspend thinking by focusing solely on the feelings evoked by
their situation. Whenever possible, we explore the bottom line:
"How does it feel?" Whenever my client and I are simultaneously interested in the bottom line, we invariably are more open
to the wisdom of our collective intuition, and when we are in
this space, our best decisions are most often made.

Our thoughts distinguish between people, objects, time and
space. Our thoughts can remove us from our experience of the

present into a conceptual perception of the past or of the future. When we examine our thoughts, we may notice that we, the examiner, are not necessarily our thoughts. We may not know where our thoughts originate, but we may begin to notice that we tend to think certain thoughts repetitively to the exclusion of other possible thoughts. Generally, our thoughts are transitory images which appear on our screen of consciousness, and when we attach significance to them, they interpret and direct our experience. Our individual bundle of thoughts define the texture and boundary of our version of reality and determine how our life unfolds.

Each thought usually has a tangible quality that can be detected by those who have opened to their feeling sensitivity. Communities of people can have their own unique collection of common thoughts which define the community's collective view of the outside world, and strangers entering their collective thought field may actually feel the communal viewpoint. Communities that share common thoughts are not necessarily confined to a particular geographical location and can be linked over great distances through established patterns of consensual thinking such as political philosophies, religions or religious beliefs.

Our reality is shaped by what we think. For example, people who think that they are not worthy of happiness usually do not achieve happiness. People who think they are victims often find themselves being victimized. People who think that all lawyers are bad will seldom meet a good one. Most of us know from personal experience that what we think is usually what we get.

Some of us may have noticed that when we forget that we are not our thoughts, our thoughts seem to automatically follow one another in a pre-programmed sequence that causes us to behave predictably, time after time. The more we let our thoughts perfunctorily control us, the more dogmatic our thinking can become. Habitual thought patterns, even in the most intelligent people, can actually prevent access to thoughts which may expand knowledge. The brilliantly innovative people of history, who broke through the envelope of what was collectively known at the time, were able to allow their minds to accept thoughts that were not otherwise available to a conditioned and limited populace.

Experiencing the awareness that we are not our thoughts can enable us to resist the temptation to become swept up by thought patterns which cause our legal relationships to unfold habitually instead of creatively. If we always think the same thoughts, we will never learn anything new or do anything differently. We might say this is absurd; we do learn new things and we do accomplish things differently than we did before. Yet, if by "new" things we mean new intentions and new attitudes and if by "new" actions we mean actions that are markedly different from our old habits, do we really think new thoughts very often? Probably not very often in a lifetime and, when we do, the change is usually triggered by dramatic events that are powerful enough to expose the fallacy of our old thoughts. We commonly characterize such events as "life changing".

Because many of us identify with and automatically act upon our thoughts, we may find it difficult to seriously entertain, much less integrate, new ways of thinking that can benefit us in our legal relationships. It is especially challenging to think, or accept, new thoughts that may help us solve a problem that was created by thinking, or accepting, our usual old thoughts. Our legal relationships often exemplify this dilemma. Many clients come to me for help in fashioning agreements that hopefully will last longer than their previous unsuccessful agreements or for help with conflicts that bear an eerie similarity to their previous conflicts.

Some of my clients have been so occupied with their typical way of thinking that they could not hear, much less accept, my suggestion that a new approach might be warranted. I have actually looked directly into clients' eyes and, to the nods of their heads, spent several minutes explaining how a new way of think-

ing could work better for them only to have them start talking
again as if I had reiterated their old position. Their usual way
of analyzing a situation was so entrenched that they could not
discern new information when it was presented to them.

I have also had to listen to clients several times before I realized that what I was hearing was new material and not on my
usual list of available options. My legally trained mind can be
a liability when it cannot create space for unfamiliar and innovative solutions.

If our legal relationships are to undertake the successful reversal
of our life patterns which have been historically exemplified by
fuzzy agreements and inevitable conflicts, we must consciously
investigate the mechanics of our thought selection and cease to
allow our thoughts to take us down old memory lanes that usually
fail to manifest our desires.

We can first acknowledge that we are not our thoughts. We can
then begin to observe our thoughts and notice which thoughts
automatically arise when we are faced with legal situations that
have similar characteristics. For example, what thoughts appear
when we encounter authority figures, when we are faced with
anger, when we are solicited by victims, when we are in the presence of the opposite sex, when we feel financially or otherwise
insecure? After we consciously round up our usual thoughts, we
can begin to exercise our will to make critical changes in our
thought selection.

We cannot simply wish certain thoughts to go away or quickly
replace them with other, more healthy thoughts. Our habitual
thoughts are not so easily dislodged from the body's neuro-
synaptical pathways. What we can more feasibly accomplish is
to implement new ways of responding to our destructive or
unhealthy thoughts. Our ability to respond in a different way, our
"response-ability", can enable us to neutralize the destructive or
unhealthy effect of our old ways of thinking.

For example, certain thought patterns may ordinarily cause us to respond with anger, jealousy, defensiveness or fear. When we see these thoughts coming in our legal relationships, we can consciously choose to respond to them without anger, jealousy, defensiveness or fear. In other words, we can let the thoughts think themselves but consciously and with willful effort refuse to let our response to them be the same old response. Instead of the anger which we know can easily make things worse, we can choose silence, temporary withdrawal or physical separation before we respond. Instead of jealousy, we can choose to honor another's right to personal freedom and reflect on how their freedom could mean more freedom for us. Instead of defensiveness, we can choose to begin our response by assuming that everything the other person has said is true. Instead of fear, we can choose to trust that everything will work out all right, especially when there is nothing we can do about it.

Altering our responses to emotionally charged thoughts will seldom happen overnight. It may take years of persistent effort to change some of our more deeply ingrained habits. Therefore, lawyers and clients can help each other consider possible alternative responses to the situations which bring them together. Each can remind the other that the instructions of the same old and powerful thought patterns may be inconsistent with the intent of the relationship and that responses which better serve that intent should be explored.

When our unhelpful thoughts trigger strong emotions, our body can also become engaged. When this happens, our tendency to identify with and follow these thoughts may then become extremely difficult to reverse. At these critical moments, we may find it useful to withdraw to a quiet place, allow our body to settle down and regain the perspective that we are not our thoughts, nor are we the emotions triggered by our thoughts. When we return to our center of balance and calmly allow our inner vision to focus on the quality of the thoughts coursing through us, we can then exercise our ability to choose a more healthy response.

Silent reflection on a legal problem can also help us imagine or receive other thoughts which are not currently available to our limited awareness. Here, silence means space between thoughts, not a lack of sound, although it is also usually helpful to be in a contemplative atmosphere without noisy distractions. Once our thoughts slow down, leaving room in between, new thoughts can begin to find their way to us. We can have that "idea that came out of the blue" which may light the path to a different response. It is not coincidental that we often get our best insights when our minds and bodies relax, for example, in the shower or in a hot bath. Therefore, when we find ourself being driven by our destructive thought patterns, we may want to literally take a shower, even if it means awkwardly excusing ourself without making any decisions. A regular meditation or relaxation practice can also be an excellent resource that can help prepare us for making sound legal decisions despite the pressure of our habitually reactive thoughts.

As we begin to contemplate and review the alternative thoughts that may be available to us when it is time to make a legal decision, we can call on our best resource, our intuition, our feeling heart. One or more of our available thoughts may simply feel right to us. This choice will usually be the one which serves the highest and best of all concerned. When we follow our heart and choose healthy responses despite unhealthy thoughts, we take another step toward consciously being responsible for the ultimate impact of our legal decisions.

Words

> The great enemy of clear language is insincerity. When there is a gap between one's real and one's declared aims, one turns, as it were, instinctively to long words and exhausted idioms, like a cuttlefish squirting out ink.
> —George Orwell, from *The Lion and the Unicorn*

> "There's glory for you!" "I don't know what you mean by 'glory'," Alice said. "I meant, there's a nice knock-down argument for you!" "But 'glory' doesn't mean 'a nice knock-down argument'," Alice objected. "When I use a word," Humpty Dumpty said in a rather scornful tone, "it means just what I choose it to mean-neither more nor less."
> —Lewis Carroll, from *Through the Looking Glass*

Even though actions may speak louder than words, spoken and written words still have tremendous power. This especially holds true in the legal system where people's fate can hinge on a single word: from the closing argument of a skilled trial lawyer to a landmark judicial decision which circumscribes conduct of people for decades, if not centuries; from a witness' answer during cross-examination to the fine print in a multi-million dollar contract.

Many lawyers pride themselves on their mastery of legal catch-words and phrases which have meaning only to the members of their professional club. Unfortunately, many lawyers learn in law school to talk over the heads of their clients. It is no wonder that there is often a vast communication gap between lawyers and clients which is seldom bridged. Many lawyers forget that they sometimes speak a foreign language and consequently fail to provide an understandable translation for their clients. When clients hear legal terminology, they may attach the wrong meaning to it or they may be too timid to ask for an explanation. When technical legal terms go unquestioned, their narrow meaning can dictate the nature and quality of the results that the relationship achieves, which may not coincide with the original intent of the parties. "Legalese" also seems to embody a morality of its own that is not necessarily consistent with intrinsic values of right and wrong. Not only do some clients fail to question lawyers about the meaning of the legal terms which define the relationship, some lawyers fail to measure parroted legal concepts against their own personal values.

Instead of blindly succumbing to a course of action simply because a lawyer cites a legal justification which apparently leaves no other choice, both the lawyer and the client can weigh the "legal" solution against their heart's discrimination between right and wrong. Each can resist the temptation to subordinate their intuition and heartfelt feelings to the rigid logic of powerful legal words. When the use of certain legal words does not harmoniously resonate with the personal values of either the lawyer or the client, open questioning of the words' literal application to the situation at hand can keep the relationship true to its intended course.

Words can also have spell-casting qualities. Some lawyers take on a client's questionable case because they are persuaded by the client's impassioned plea. Similarly, a client can be led to take an undesirable course of legal action simply because a lawyer says it is the right thing to do. People who are articulate, who have a "way" with words, often use their gift to persuade others. In legal relationships, this power of persuasion can also manifest as manipulation.

The distinction between persuasion and manipulation is a fine line but essential to grasp. Persuasion is the effort to convince another that a particular belief should be adopted. The persuader is usually motivated by an inner conviction that the belief can benefit the person adopting it. Manipulation also involves convincing another to adopt a particular belief, but the manipulator has no such sense of conviction and does not value the belief except for its use in controlling another for the manipulator's personal gain.

It is possible for a listener to determine whether the apparently uncontroverted logic of the speaker's words is coming from a persuader or a manipulator. If we focus on the words alone, it may be extremely difficult for us to make this distinction in the presence of the person because the words may be deliberately designed to keep our feelings at a distance. However, by noticing the person's demeanor, tone of voice, gestures or other nonverbal communication, we may get in touch with an intuitive feeling which can unmask the speaker's purpose.

Even a skilled manipulator may reveal his or her true colors through a "slip of the tongue". When a slip occurs, it should not be ignored. Any attempt to cover up the slip, whether by joking or saying, "I didn't mean that", does not have to divert us from sifting the literal meaning of the words used in the "slip" through our "crap detector". These "slips" may not be slips at all but may be glimpses of what is behind the manipulator's smoke screen.

Some manipulators do not consciously know that they manipulate others. Verbal manipulation can also be described as seductive behavior and may be entirely habitual. Habitual or not, manipulation in a legal relationship can block the parties' mutual clarity of intent and can impede successful achievement of the relationship's purpose.

Each word we utter can reflect our inner intent and translate it into sound vibrations. The frequencies of these vibrations transmit our intent to others who then determine whether or not there is a corresponding resonance with their own inner intent. When the sound vibrations are manipulated to disguise a person's true inner intent, experienced listeners can often detect the subtleties of their inherent disharmony. The resonating chord within the listener may have a flat or atonal quality to it. Literally, manipulative words may not "ring true" nor "sound right".

Once we begin to listen to our inner tuning forks and thereby heighten our powers of discernment, we may be able to discern where the speaker is coming from and can then choose either to move toward or away from a relationship with this person.

If we choose to move toward relationship, we can then come to terms with our own choice of vocabulary. We cannot call attention to the verbal manipulation of others while we ignore our own tendency to manipulate with words, especially in a legal context where success or failure may turn on the meaning of a single word.

Words used glibly or casually without the force of strong conviction or conscious intent can have the same effect as words used to deliberately manipulate. Attaining the successful manifestation of our intent may require us to substitute consciously chosen language for idle chatter, misplaced cliches, cynical jokes, sexual innuendos or other habitual verbal distractions. We can carefully and deliberately choose words which will incrementally move us closer to the fulfillment of the purpose of our legal relationship. Not only can our words be consistent with the achievement of our goals, our success may ultimately depend upon their honesty and compassion. When we ignore the integrity and consequences of our means, the end may be fundamentally flawed.

Action

Our deeds determine us, as much as we
determine our deeds; and until we know what
has been or will be the peculiar combination of
outward with inward facts, which constitute a
man's critical actions, it will be better not to
think ourselves wise about his character.
—George Eliot, from *Adam Bede*

It was a high counsel that I once heard given to
a young person, 'Always do what you are afraid
to do.'
—Ralph Waldo Emerson, "Heroism", from
Essays

Pooh began to feel a little more comfortable,
because when you are a Bear of Very Little
Brain, and you Think of Things, you find
sometimes that a Thing which seemed very
Thingish inside you is quite different when it
gets out into the open and has other people
looking at it.
—A.A. Milne, from *The House at Pooh
Corner*

I can remember many social discussions when I have eloquently
defended some of the great legal principles fundamental to our
way of life only to later fail to apply them in my daily practice
of law. It was easy for me to talk but difficult for me to act.

Even though our legal relationships may be blessed with pure
intent, focused thoughts and speech that clearly expresses the two,
all is for naught unless we can "walk our talk". Our words and
our attitude are often baby steps taken by our intent into the outer
world. What usually propels our inner vision into physical
manifestation is our action.

Most of what we communicate to one another in our legal relationships is non-verbal. Conversely, our ability to listen is not necessarily limited to our capacity to hear. Many of us have an innate ability to detect a hypocrite, a person who says one thing and does another. Most of us have the capacity to develop this skill if we learn to concentrate on how a person acts instead of on what a person says. In order for us to be able to identify inconsistencies between another person's words and actions, we must also be able to recognize when our own behavior belies the words we use. When we achieve this state of awareness, we can then deal with another's hypocrisy as well as our own.

We can learn a great deal about our own integrity from how we act. We always know when we are not being true to our innermost feelings. Obvious examples are when we think one thing and yet say another, when we want to say "no" but we say "yes", when we don't like what is going on but we go along.

When the direction of our energy is inconsistent with the course envisioned by our heart's intent and the aspiration of our corresponding thoughts, the inconsistency can often appear in the physical body as a state of "dis-ease". We may feel "ill at ease" because we have fallen short of our internal measure of who we are.

If we know what actions we should be taking, then why do we ever choose actions which lead us away from our heart's intent? The reasons are too innumerable to mention here, but most of the explanations have "fear" in common, a fear that is so powerful that it can immobilize us at the precise moment we begin to act. This fear can cause us to believe that our action will backfire and result in devastating humiliation. Such fear can overpower our desire to act upon our feelings when it springs from a shame-based belief that we are defective and therefore do not deserve to be ourselves.

In order to begin to choose legal actions which effectively implement our heartfelt intent and to "feel better" about ourselves, we must have faith that we can actually survive how others might respond to our actions. We can also realize that any alteration of our behavior in anticipation of the reaction of others may cause our body to experience symptoms of physical congestion or discomfort. We may literally feel "sick" when we fail to do the right thing.

With these concepts in mind, we can also identify emotional mechanisms that thwart our desire to enact ourselves, to be who we really are, to be the right stuff. Although sifting through emotional layers may reveal behavioral patterns originally designed to protect us from abuse or shame, we may find that the toggle switch that blocks the flow from the center of our being is a terror that our action will be negatively judged.

Some of us may need the guidance of a professional therapist to help us break our habits, but at some point along the way, each of us can acknowledge that we have to face our inner dragon alone. We can muster our courage with psychological tools that we learn from others, but when the moment to choose a course of action finally comes, no one can make the choice for us. Either we act with courage or we cower in fear. When we stop feeling sorry for ourselves and care less about what anyone else might think, we may discover that there was never anything to fear in the first place, because our expectation of shame was only a ghost from our past resurrected by our conditioned mind. We may have created these holographs at a time when they might have been useful, but now they can only limit us as we recreate who we are. We can now finally accept that it makes no difference if our actions are criticized by others, just as Picasso was not for everyone. As we courageously and methodically choose legal courses of action that serve to illuminate our highest and best intent, our fear of criticism from others may slowly loosen its grip.

When we conscientiously practice the full expression of who we are, we may discover that our purposeful intent, right attitude, complementary thought development, conscious word selection and willful action become indistinguishable concepts. When we totally trust our intuition, our action will be virtually spontaneous. When we act spontaneously, directly from our heart, we will always be honest. Such a display of honesty will usually sound a resonant chord in the hearts of others and, even if they disagree with the message, they will respect the messenger.

In the context of legal relationships, our actions are not only a litmus test of our integrity; they also determine the measure of success the legal relationship can achieve. Because words enjoy such a prominent place in the law, their logical and technical use can sometimes disguise actions which do not implement the intent of the parties. When the words used by a lawyer or a client, although replete with unquestionable logic, begin to sound flat to our inner listening device, we may find it helpful to imagine what action is being suggested by the discordant words. If we feel that the suggested outcome may not comport fully with our intent, we can interrupt the speaker and demand action that is as purposeful as it is "legal".

This may be a challenging task for a client faced with a lawyer weaned on a legal dictionary. Fear of sounding stupid has to be overcome. Failure to risk stupidity at this point can ensure an unsatisfactory result. When in doubt, the client can say "no" to words used by the lawyer which dilute or divert the client's intent.

Similarly, when a sophisticated client wants a lawyer to spin a web of legalese to disguise action that is dishonest, morally corrupt or incongruent with the lawyer's personal sense of what is right or fair, the lawyer can dispel his or her fear of being rejected or of losing a paying client by squeezing out the simple word "no." Once this word is out of the mouth, there is no turning back, and only right action will suffice.

A legal relationship is the sum of its parties. Lawyer and client must both find the courage to act with integrity within the relationship. Only then can the two direct their coordinated action outward from the relationship to manifest success. Not only do each of us have to struggle to break through our own layers of limitation and temerity, we can help each other understand that we cannot accept it any other way. When we meet resistance from our lawyer or our client who feels threatened by our determination to act with unbending integrity, we can remember the difficulty of our own process and have compassion for the other person's reluctance to take the leap of faith. As compassionate as we may be, however, we cannot let the other's hesitation deter us from completing the full cycle of our own metamorphosis. We may hear arguments for the usual, safe way of doing things that will be extremely convincing and enticing, precisely because the usual way is safe and entails no risk of rejection or criticism. If we take the bait however, we are lost, at least for the moment. Our chance to act with integrity will have passed once again, and in future moments, we will have to contend with the consequences of our failure to assert our true self.

A lawyer and a client may purify their intent, hone their attitudes and eliminate their negative words and thoughts, yet such is all for naught unless their actions correspond with precision accuracy. Consistent actions are the essential follow-through to legal decision-making. Even though we may have chosen a new script, our bodies may automatically reenact scenes out of our negative past unless we actually move our bodies through physical postures that demonstrate our commitment to a more positive way of relating. For example, even though we may desire to transform our anger and actually select a new way of responding to an event that normally incites our anger, our inner victory is meaningless if we deliver the new response with a cynical twist or if we offer forgiveness in a condescending manner.

Even if we do totally commit to change, our old thought forms may continue to arise and may never totally disappear, but the more times we can change our responses through willful and committed action, our old ways of thinking can begin to exert less and less control over our lives.

For lawyers and clients to engage in ground-breaking, deliberate action, courage is required. The easy part is to suspend years of rigid and deeply ingrained thinking while we contemplate unfamiliar and even wildly innovative alternatives. The hardest part is to convert our newly formed thoughts into action. It is not enough to write a new mental script; we have to act it out.

If our hearts are committed to the task, we can pull it off. If we do not really believe in the legal course we have chosen, our efforts to act may be "half-hearted", and we will likely fall short of our goal. Only when we act courageously, despite our fear of failure, despite our fear of the unknown, despite our fear of judgment from others, can we experience positive change in our legal relationships.

Transformation of our legal relationships, as well as our legal system, cannot begin to occur unless and until we are willing to "trans" or change the "form" of our actions from the usual, the mundane, the rational to the intuitive, the feeling, the integral. This can happen when we sharpen our awareness, align with our essence and liberate our courage. It is more than a coincidence that the word "courage" is derived from the Latin word "cor" which means "heart".

The challenge is individual yet also interpersonal. We can help others through the door of legal transformation by our example. Our courage to act can inspire others to act, even though that cannot be our main concern. If we act solely for others, we have missed the point. We must put ourselves first in order to break the behavioral ties that bind us to mediocrity. The operative paradox is that others can be helped only if we are indulgently selfish. Isn't it about time?

Measuring Success

> To travel hopefully is a better thing than to
> arrive, and the true success is to labour.
> —Robert Louis Stevenson, "Aes Triplex", from
> *Virginibus Puerisque*
>
> She knows there's no success like failure
> And that failure's no success at all.
> —Bob Dylan, from "Love Minus Zero/No
> Limit"

Following my initiation as a defender of indigent juveniles and adults charged with criminal offenses, I counseled many people over the years concerning the gamut of legal challenges, including business agreements, employment matters, banking law, corporate and partnership formation and dissolution, the prosecution and defense of commercial lawsuits, adoption and guardianship, copyright and trademark protection, marriage and divorce, personal injury law, medical and legal malpractice, bankruptcy, non-profit organizations, probate and conservatorships, estate and trust planning and real estate transactions. I could easily choose to measure the success of all of these relationships in terms of whether or not my clients got what they were after, from winning a lawsuit to winning a negotiation to winning certification that they technically complied with the law. However, as I reflect back over the years, I realize that the win-loss measuring tape only accounts for a single dimension of the multi-dimensional concept of success.

Success means "the satisfactory attainment of a desired object or end." I have known many clients who won the dispute, won the negotiation or won technical compliance yet were left feeling unfulfilled and incomplete. In almost every case, each of these

141

clients discovered that what they got was not really what they wanted, at least not all of what they wanted.

Most of us have heard stories about pyrrhic legal victories. The divorced spouse gets all of the assets of the marriage but has no relationship with her children's father. The business executive gets all of the power over, but no respect from, his new employee. The corporate board gets an exemption from compliance with federal pollution regulations but loses the confidence of its environmentally conscious customers. Obviously, legal success is not necessarily winning, because winning may turn out not to be the object of our desire.

There is no specific formula for calculating how much success we are enjoying in our legal relationships. So how can we tell if we are on the right path? The answer may be paradoxical. The more we follow our heart's desire by acting upon our intuition, the more our success is likely to defy the logic that winning must be at the expense of someone.

Since our new commitment to our intuition may not be quickly welcomed by many of our peers, we may have to settle for success by perseverance. We cannot waver from our heart's purpose even though our mind may not be convinced of success and, in fact, is sure of failure. We can trust that when we remain steadfast to our truth beyond our mind's fear-imposed limits on the possible, the apparition of failure will dissolve. We can also have faith that those who may initially have a negative reaction to our new expression of feelings in our legal relationships may ultimately acknowledge our view of what is right even if only as an exception to their general rule. Lawyers and clients who are not fully committed to follow their own feelings will inwardly admire our courage and may even find a way to accommodate us if we stand resolute for what we know to be right.

As we continue to practice our expression of who we are, we may not have to wait until the final result of our legal endeavors to know that we are on the right track. It is possible for us to develop the ability to detect early signs which validate our intuition and which can help fine-tune our heart's guidance system. As our awareness heightens, we may also notice synchronistic events which alert us to the necessity of reevaluating our intent or our chosen course of action.

These signals may appear from anywhere within our internal or external environment. Our ability to detect them depends upon our capacity to notice or observe what is happening inside and outside of our bodies in any given moment without being distracted by thoughts which recall the past or attempt to predict the future. When we maintain a state of mind which is not predisposed to judge what appears before it, we can begin to notice our intuitive response to what we are noticing. It is these feelings that can tell us whether or not we are on the right path. In fact, we may also begin to notice that the outer signals and the inner feelings are virtually indistinguishable and mysteriously seem to emanate from the same source. The more that we are able to open our awareness to the present, the more we may experience the paradox that all things are simultaneously separated *and* integrated.

In order for us to attain a state of consciousness in our legal relationships which can help us gauge the rightness of our course, we may find it useful to detach ourselves, at least for the moment, from any emotional investment in our point of view or our desired outcome. When we consciously practice releasing our attachment to any result, we may gain enough perspective to notice if our present intent, attitude, thoughts, words and behavior are truly serving us.

Real success is a state of being that feels good about the choices that are being made, when our actions reflect our honest commitment to a clear intent. Results which are inconsistent with our efforts to align ourselves with our true nature may indicate that we have denied the calling of our core feelings. Incomplete or impaired results can usually be traced to our limited vision, confused thoughts or half-hearted action. The degree of our success is directly proportional to the extent we honor our feelings and act on our intuition.

Which human experiences cause us to feel "good"? When our spirits are "lifted" or "uplifted", we feel good. When we are in the presence of beauty or feel beautiful, we feel good. When we experience happiness or joy, we feel good. When our legal endeavors evoke these feelings, either in ourselves or in others, we can say that our efforts have also been "successful".

If we know that upliftment, beauty and joy are characteristics that are often associated with the realization of success, then why can't we redefine what we want to achieve through our legal relationships in these terms? Why can't the goal of our legal decision-making process be "upliftment"? Why can't it be "beauty"? Why not "joy"?

Imagine the possibilities if a lawyer and a client weighed legal options in terms of the degree of joy each would bring? Wouldn't the criteria for the selection of a legal alternative be different if our goal was upliftment or beauty instead of winning or profit?

When we measure success in these terms, or at least give these qualities some consideration and chart our legal course accordingly, we can liberate our intuition to explore solutions that our mind would otherwise reject as "impractical" or "frivolous".

When we let our good feelings flow through our bodies and into expression, we actually experience a pleasant physical sensation. When we block, suppress or deny this flow, our bodies react accordingly, and the physical experience is usually uncomfortable, if not downright unpleasant. When we feel good about having done the right thing, regardless of whether or not we notch another victory on our competitive belt, we will always be able to describe our encounter with the legal system as a positive one. Our society needs more of these success stories.

Sacrifice and Service

Lord, make me an instrument of Your peace!
Where there is hatred let me sow love;
Where there is injury, pardon;
Where there is doubt, faith;
Where there is despair, hope;
Where there is darkness, light;
Where there is sadness, joy.
O divine Master, grant that I may not so much
   seek
To be consoled as to console;
To be understood as to understand;
To be loved as to love.
For it is in giving that we receive;
It is in pardoning that we are pardoned;
And it is in dying that we are born to eternal
   life.
   —St. Francis of Assisi

When we are determined to fully engage our intuition and compassion in all of our legal relationships, not only with our lawyer
or our client but also with our prospective partner, competitor
or adversary, we may want to reflect upon the quality of the service that we want to provide for others and the extent to which
we are willing to sacrifice for it.

In 1993, I received a telephone call from an old friend who
is a lawyer in Wyoming. He wanted me to represent a man who
had been sexually molested by a Catholic priest when he was a
young boy growing up in northern New Mexico. Since the lawsuit was to be brought against the Catholic Church in New
Mexico, my friend asked me to serve as local counsel. We soon
learned that other members of our client's family and childhood
community had also been sexually abused by the same priest. We

then filed multiple lawsuits in Albuquerque.

It soon became apparent that we were participating in an historical exposure of the moral corruption and abuse of power within the Church. I began to focus on my indispensable role in history with self-righteous aplomb. I was going to make sure that the Church was crucified with its own hypocrisy in a public trial. The truth about the Church had to be told, and I had been chosen to tell it.

I was wrong. What we were doing was important, and very necessary, but when I became personally attached to the historical significance of what we were doing, I lost sight of the real purpose of my service and was moving in a direction that would harm, not help, my clients.

Fortunately, I woke up before I caused any serious damage. When the Church's lawyer approached us in an effort to settle our clients' claims, I wanted to advise all of my clients to reject this settlement overture and to press ahead with the litigation in order to exact a full measure of retribution for the unspeakable agony my clients had suffered throughout the years. When all of my clients did not enthusiastically respond to my aggressive approach, my intuitive voice suggested that my moral outrage, even though justified, was not necessarily serving my clients' best interests.

My clients had been horribly abused, and most of them needed to heal in private, not be subjected to the further trauma of a trial and its attendant publicity. I had allowed my egocentric desires to interfere with my ability to effectively serve my clients' needs. I had to give up my personal investment in the outcome and tune in to what most of my clients really wanted, reasonably fair compensation and healing solitude.

When I finally let go to selfless service and sacrificed my ego's attachment to a particular result, my clients breathed a collective sigh of relief, and their confidence in me was restored.

I am not ego bashing here. I am only suggesting that a lawyer will find it difficult to truly understand and communicate with a client unless the ego is sacrificed. All of the ego's desires and fears that will personalize or manipulate a particular legal result must give way to selfless attention to what the client really wants. After the ego has bowed in deference to the real desires of the client, the lawyer can then intuit the appropriate service. The right service may require the lawyer to again pick up the sword of the ego. Many clients seek help from lawyers because they lack the egoic strength to help themselves. In such cases, the lawyer's ego can become a vital and necessary part of successful service.

I have handled several lawsuits which I could not settle for the client, no matter how hard I tried. In each of these cases, I personally desired the case to settle without going to trial. I wanted to avoid having to devote myself to the rigors and time demands of a trial. However, the harder I pushed for settlement, the more obvious it became that these cases were destined for trial. I intuitively knew that these cases should be tried, yet my self-interests caused me to push for settlement. In each of these cases, I finally surrendered to my intuition and prepared for trial. When I gave up on the settlement that should never have occurred anyway, I could become fully aligned with the task of providing my client with the best representation possible. My surrender led to service for my client and beyond.

Sacrifice is not necessarily taking a vow of poverty, forsaking our individual needs or the needs of our family, nor abandoning our sense of who we are. Sacrifice is the humble embrace of the paradox of life, that we are all separate yet unified, apart yet together. When we accept the yin with the yang, we consciously surrender to what is, instead of unconsciously acquiescing to what is not.

Service is something we give to another that can help alleviate their suffering. Service is compassion, and suffering is the illusion of separateness. Service is not necessarily helping someone make a lot of money, climb the corporate ladder or beat an opponent. Service is supporting another person in their search for truth, not using them to advance our own cause. Service can be performed without rescue and without disregarding healthy interpersonal boundaries.

Service and sacrifice originate in the heart. They cannot be conceived by the mind because they are concepts that defy logic, and they can only be understood and experienced by our feeling intuition. When we commit to sacrifice and service in our legal relationships, we not only contribute to the recovery of the legal system, we embark on our own personal journey of healing self-discovery.

5

Where to From Here?

...The times are fearfully heavy. For several
years now, we have entered a total Middle
Ages. Wars, shadows, hatred, pogroms, they're
all there. There are still a few magnificent,
fiery hearts left, but without any tangible
results. What is our duty? To remain faithful to
the Flame. At present, it remains hidden,
infirm, diffident. But the time will come when
it shall rule again upon this awesome,
marvelous earth. We must remain strong, Leah,
and faithful; this is the only salvation. Our cry
in the desert today will later on once again
change stones to men. There is something in
the human heart that can never be extinguished,
and this something is our only hope....
—Nikos Kazantzakis, writing to his wife in
1938, from *Nikos Kazantzakis, A Biography*
by Helen Kazantzakis

The concepts and suggestions offered here are not absolute. They
arise from my personal experience and may help stimulate useful discussion among lawyers and clients and may even lead to
more positive legal relationships that enhance the quality of our
legal system.

The task before us is not easy nor is it uncomplicated. Changes
in our legal relationships cannot occur overnight. There is no
quick fix. The legal system will initially resist the consideration
of intuitive feelings in legal decision-making. Advocating an
introduction of the heart may be difficult to articulate to a status
quo conditioned to receive information only through rational and

linear channels.

So why bother? Because the alternative to bothering is more of the same dysfunction, more of the same disappointment, more of the same failure. We can no longer tolerate unsavory legal relationships which destroy more than they preserve, which denigrate instead of elevate. We are tired of dishonesty and manipulation. We are fed up with rigid logic and the ridicule of emotion. We long to relate to others without ulterior motives. We want to experience harmony and peace, instead of acrimony and bitterness. The attitude of selfish "loopholism" is eroding our moral fabric and jeopardizing our quality of life, and our hearts ache to restore the balance.

We must remember that we can only effect change in our immediate environment. The focus must literally be from moment to moment. Clinging to the past or looking toward the future may divert our energy and attention from the task at hand. We can only work on ourselves and our relationships with individual determination and trust that the rest of the world will take care of itself.

Our aim is for balance between the best of our mind and the best of our heart. In restoring our heart to its full capacity, we cannot lock our mind in the cellar. If there is a close call, we may want to give the nod to the message from the heart because we have a lot of dysfunctional history to overcome, yet we should avoid any overcompensation which will exclude the mind's valuable talents.

Our legal system and the legal relationships within it are mutually creative. Each defines itself by the structure of the other. Each legal relationship therefore contains within it a microcosmic template of the larger and seemingly intractable legal system from which the legal system can be recreated and upon which it depends for its existence. In other words, the whole is the part and the part is the whole, each reflecting the essence of the other. Once we begin to realize that the health of the entire legal system is totally dependent upon and directly affected by every single legal relationship unfolding within it, we can absolutely trust that each transformative step we take as individuals will positively alter the system within which we operate. Acquiescence to any perception of what we believe the legal system to be simply insures the perpetuation of that perception. We cannot escape our individual responsibility.

When we finally accept full responsibility for ourselves and for the health of each of our legal relationships, we can then begin to allow our intuitive heart to do its healing work, and the legal system will naturally reflect the results.

References and Suggested Reading

American Bar Association, "The Report of At the Breaking Point, a National Conference on the Emerging Crisis in the Quality of Lawyers' Health and Lives-Its Impact on Law Firms and Client Services," April 5-6, 1991.

Bly, Robert, *Iron John: A Book About Men*, Addison Wesley Publishing, 1990

Bly, Robert, *A Little Book on the Human Shadow*, ed. by William Booth, Harper San Francisco, 1988

Bradshaw, John, *Bradshaw On: The Family*, Health Communications, Inc., 1988

Bradshaw, John, *Healing the Shame That Binds You*, Health Communications, Inc., 1988

Campbell, Joseph, *Hero With a Thousand Faces*, Princeton University Press, 1949

Chopra, Deepak, M.D., *Quantum Healing: Exploring the Frontiers of Mind/Body Medicine*, Bantam Books, 1989

Chopra, Deepak, *The Seven Spiritual Laws of Success*, Amber-Allen/New World Library, 1995

Covey, Stephen R., *The Seven Habits of Highly Effective People*, Simon & Schuster, 1989

The Dalai Lama, *A Flash of Lightning in the Night: A Guide to the Bodhisattva's Way of Life*, Shambhala, 1994.

The Dalai Lama, *Essential Teachings*, North Atlantic Books, 1995

Dass, Ram and Gorman, Paul, *How Can I Help?*, Alfred A. Knopf, 1991

Estes, Clarissa Pinkola, Ph.D., *Women Who Run With the Wolves*, Ballantine Books, 1992.

Ferguson, Marilyn, *The Aquarian Conspiracy: Personal & Social Transformation*, revised edition, J.P. Tarcher, 1987

The Fourteenth Dalai Lama, *Kindness, Clarity and Insight*, Snow Lion Publications, 1984

Hengstler, Gary A., "Vox Populi, The Public Perception of Lawyers: ABA Poll", *American Bar Association Journal*, September 1993.

Hillman, James, *The Thought of the Heart & the Soul of the World*, Spring Publications, Inc., 1992

Johnson, Robert A., *He: Understanding Masculine Psychology*, revised edition, Harper & Row, 1989

Johnson, Robert A., *Owning Your Own Shadow*, Harper San Francisco, 1991

Johnson, Robert A., *She: Understanding Feminine Psychology*, revised edition, Harper Perennial, 1989

Jung, Carl, *Man and His Symbols*, Doubleday, 1964

Jung, Carl, *Memories, Dreams, Reflections*, Random House, 1989

Jung, Carl, *The Portable Jung*, ed. by Joseph Campbell, Penguin Books, 1971

Jung, Carl, *Synchronicity: An Acausal Connecting Principle*, Princeton University Press, 1973

Kaufman, Gershen, Ph.D., *Shame: The Power of Caring*, Schenkman Books, Inc., 1980

Kornfield, Jack, *A Path With Heart*, Bantam Books, 1993

Maharshi, Ramana, *The Collected Works of Ramana Maharshi*, ed. by Arthur Osborne, Samuel Weiser, Inc., 1970

Miller, Alice, *For Your Own Good*, trans. by Hildegarde and Hunter Hannum, The Noonday Press, 1990

Moore, Thomas, *Care of the Soul*, Harper Collins, 1992

Muller, Wayne, *Legacy of the Heart*, Simon & Schuster, 1992

Rinpoche, Kalu, *The Chariot for Traveling the Path to Freedom*, Khagyu Dharma, 1985

Rinpoche, Kalu, *The Dharma*, State University of New York Press, 1986

Spence, Gerry, Chapters 2, 5, 13 and 14 of *How to Argue and Win Every Time*, St. Martin's Press, 1995

Schultz, Ron, *Unconventional Wisdom: Twelve Remarkable Innovators Tell How Intuition Can Revolutionize Decisionmaking*, Harper Business, 1994

Singer, June, *Boundaries of the Soul: The Practice of Jung's Psychology*, Doubleday, 1953

Steiner, Rudolph, *The Essential Steiner*, ed. by Robert A. McDermott, Harper & Row, 1984

Steiner, Rudolph, *Theosophy*, Anthroposophic Press, Inc., 1971

Tavris, Carol, *Anger: The Misunderstood Emotion*, Simon & Schuster, 1982

Wilber, Ken (ed.), *The Holographic Paradigm and Other Paradoxes*, Shambhala Publications, Inc., 1985

Wilber, Ken, *No Boundary: Eastern and Western Approaches to Personal Growth*, Shambhala Publications, Inc., 1981

Woodman, Marion, *Addiction to Perfection*, Inner City Books, 1982

Yogananda, Paramahansa, *Autobiography of a Yogi*, Self-Realization Fellowship, 1973

About the Author

Merit graduated from the U.S. Air Force Academy in 1969. He received a Masters Degree from the University of Colorado in 1972 and a Juris Doctor Degree from the Washington College of Law at The American University in Washington, D.C., in 1975. He practiced law in Colorado from 1975 until he moved to New Mexico in 1986. His professional career has included the practice of criminal law, corporation and partnership law, contract and real estate law, family law, estate planning and commercial and personal injury litigation. He is an experienced trial lawyer and handles cases in State and Federal courts. Merit is now practicing in Santa Fe in the fields of personal injury and professional malpractice, with an emphasis on sexual abuse litigation.

Index

abuse, 20
action(s), 51, 121, 123, 127, 131, 135-138
agreement(s), 50, 78-79, 89
anger, 70-71, 108, 110-120
archetype(s), 45, 58, 60-62

boundary(ies), 92-93, 96-97, 101, 111, 113, 148

competition, 53-56, 73, 101
conflict, 29, 56, 110-115, 128
consciousness, 14, 56, 126
corporation(s), 48-52

denial, 29, 40-43, 72, 91, 95, 104
dispute(s), 70-75, 110

forgiveness, 116-120

hero warrior, 58-62

intuition, 30, 41-42, 66, 103-104, 107, 123, 125, 130, 132, 138

morality, 19, 105, 132

projection(s), 9-15, 20-22, 24, 33, 38, 66, 95, 96

rescue(r), 32-35, 38, 65, 72, 95

sacrifice, 82, 145, 147-148
shadow(s), 17-24, 33, 59, 60, 95, 96
shame, 26-30, 32, 136, 137
synchronicity, 154
synchronistic, 13,143

technology, 60,104
therapist, 13,137

victim(s), 31-35, 46, 70, 72, 95, 113-114, 126

win-win, 56-57, 73, 79, 122
witch(es), 22-25

ORDER FORM

*Phone, fax or write if you would like a copy of our catalog
which lists all books, videos, etc. that we produce and distribute.*

Telephone orders: Call 505-474-0998
to charge to Visa, MC, AE or Discover
Fax orders: 505-471-2584

Mail orders: The Message Company
4 Camino Azul
Santa Fe, NM 87505

CODE #	AUTHOR	TITLE	QTY	PRICE	TOTAL
020268	Willis Harman, PhD	Spirituality in Business: The Tough Questions Color video, 60 minutes	____	19.95	____
020276	Richard Barrett	Unfolding of the World Bank Spiritual Unfoldment Society Color video, 60 minutes	____	19.95	____
020284	Sharon Morgen	Exploring the New Paradigm in Sales Color Video, 120 minutes	____	29.95	____
020292		Buying Facilitation: The Service that Sells Color video, 60 minutes	____	19.95	____
020306	Martin Rutte	Livelihood: Growing Spirit at Work Color video, 60 minutes	____	19.95	____
D20314	Judith Thompson, PhD	Moving from Corporate Social Responsibility to Corporate Spirituality Color video, 60 minutes	____	19.95	____
D20322	Michael Horst and Brooke Warrick	Spirituality in Real Estate Color video, 60 minutes	____	19.95	____
D20373	Ted Nicholas	Why 97% of our Conventional Wisdom is Wrong and How to Change it Color video, 120 minutes	____	29.95	____
D20381		Success in Life is Found in Balance Color video, 60 minutes	____	19.95	____
D20403		The Crucial Difference Between Positive and Negative Selfishness Color video, 60 minutes	____	19.95	____
D20411		Examining 17 Areas of your Belief System Color video, 120 minutes	____	29.95	____

Subtotal: ____

USA shipping: 2.00

Extra shipping: ____

NM residents add 5.75% sales tax: ____

Total: ____

Extra shipping charges:
• Priority mail: add $3.00
• AK, HI, Canada: add 10%
• All other countries: add 25%
• Foreign Air: add $8.00 per tape

❏ Enclosed is a check/money order for total
❏ Please charge to my ❏ Visa ❏ MC ❏ AE ❏ Discover

Card # _____ Expiration Date: _____

Signature _____

Name _____ Address _____

City/Sate/Province_____ Zip/Postal Code _____

Phone: _____

ORDER FORM

Phone, fax or write if you would like a copy of our catalog listing
all books, videos, etc. that we produce and distribute.

Telephone Orders: Call 505-474-0998   **Mail Orders:** The Message Company
to charge your VISA, MasterCard,   4 Camino Azul
American Express or Discover   Santa Fe, NM 87505
Fax Orders: 505-471-2584

CODE	TITLE	QUANTITY	PRICE	TOTAL
D20004	**Law and the Heart: A Practical Guide for Successful Lawyer/Client Relationships** 168 pages, 5^1/$_2$ x 8^1/$_2$, paper back.	_____ x	$14.95 =	_____
D20128	**How to Find the Best Lawyers ... and Save 50% on Legal Fees** 200 pages, 5^1/$_2$ x 8^1/$_2$, paper back.	_____ x	$14.95 =	_____
D20101	**History of the American Constitutional or Common Law** 144 pages, 8^1/$_2$ x 11, paperback.	_____ x	$11.95 =	_____
D20020	**The Physics of Love** 156 pages, 8^1/$_2$ x 11, paperback.	_____ x	$15.95 =	_____
D20063	**Spiritual Vampires: The Use and Misuse of Spiritual Power** 256 pages, 6 x 9, paperback.	_____ x	$14.95 =	_____
D2008X	**Nikola Tesla's Earthquake Machine** 176 pages, 8^1/$_2$ x 11, paperback.	_____ x	$16.95 =	_____
D20039	**Universal Laws Never Before Revealed: Keely's Secrets** 288 pages, 8^1/$_2$ x 11, paperback.	_____ x	$19.95 =	_____
D20055	**International Directory of Hemp Products and Suppliers** 144 pages, 6 x 9, paperback.	_____ x	$29.95 =	_____
D20047	**Grazing Through the Woods with the Herb Man** Color video.	_____ x	$19.95 =	_____

Extra Shipping Charges:
• Priority Mail: add $3.00
• AK, HI, Canada: add 10%
• All other countries: add 25%
• Foreign Air: add $8.00 per book

SUBTOTAL _____

SHIPPING $2.00

NM RES. ADD SALES TAX 5.75% _____

TOTAL $_____

❏ Enclosed is a check or money order for total.
❏ Please charge to my [ ] VISA [ ] MC
  [ ] American Express [ ] Discover

NAME _____

CARD # _____

ADDRESS _____

EXP. DATE _____

CITY / STATE / ZIP _____

SIGNATURE _____

PHONE _____